Flickers
of
Light
Love
and
Air

Original poems by

TWILA JESSOP

ISBN 978-1-64028-628-3 (Paperback)
ISBN 978-1-64028-629-0 (Digital)

Christian Faith Publishing, Inc.
296 Chestnut Street
Meadville, PA 16335
www.christianfaithpublishing.com

Printed in the United States of America

Love and Air

This be my prayer
That God supply me love and air
And wherever follow I my feet
May love and air remain so sweet

Purpose

Father of fortune, maker of dreams
Spin me a vision of purpose in things
Guide me to where my best work will be
Awaken my soul that I may serve Thee

No Doubt

I felt you standing near to me
Although you weren't seen
I asked myself if this could be
More than a lovely dream

Old age, we're trapped in pupae stage
Before our wings can sprout
So never feel discouraged
And never have a doubt

Layers

As the layers fly off and some simply fall
The stains and the dirt peel away
And some that are torn from this crusty old wall
Try to cling to their old faulty ways

The Light that once strained to see through the stains
Now shines much more brightly and clear
A crystal clear heart is now what remains
Now washed and made new with the tears

Final Season

Her clear blue eyes were fading
As she went from youth to crone
The angels all were waiting
So she was not alone

The years did treat her kindly
'Midst the laughter and the tears
And peace would be hers finally
In the music of the spheres

I Was Once Among You

There soon will be a crossroad
In the days of all our lives
And you have carried your load
But soon it's time to die

So what now did you carry
Was it dirt or was it gold
And if you chose to tarry
We'll all be growing old

Was your burden very heavy
Was your cross too much to bear
Did your feet stay strong and steady
Did you see me standing there

For I was once among you
As the living not the dead
I was black and then a Jew
And then Protestant instead

Now I sit beside you
You don't even turn your head
And I wonder if you ever knew
My heart for you had bled

You would listen to the whisper
As my heart reached out for yours
Yours would say you missed her
Though I'm here right by the door

We never really leave those
That live inside our hearts
And love is like a tender rose
So soon to fall apart

Then another door is open
And on the other side
The words that we have spoken
In a thousand other lives

The people we have loved there
All waiting for us now
The love that we had once shared
Lives on within our brow

And as we think about them
They appear before our eyes
Embrace them like that long lost friend
We laugh until we cry

Though we needn't think about that
For the magic to appear
We needn't strain at pesky gnat
We needn't live with fear

Yes, I was once among you
In another time and place
As surely as the sky is blue
I surely know your face

Drifted

If we could just see past the bend in the road
We'd see what our future may be
If we have a friend to help carry the load
We'd sail through eternity

The load may have shifted, will he be true
Or will he have drifted to shades not true blue
Shall we all meet by the fork in the road
Will we all wonder has this been foretold

Though we hold a high standard, it may not be fair
Can we all be so holy and wise
But look 'round the corner, I'll look for you there
I'll see by the depth in your eyes

So walk with me, brother, my sister, my friend
Walk with me, daughter and son, to the end
Guide me, my father, my mother, my love
Help me to rise to the love from above

Oasis

An oasis stood before me
In a world so upside down
My tears had made me thirsty
And I thought that I might drown

A fountain just appeared where
What had been barren ground
Somehow my life has lead here
As I circled all around

In youth I was expectant
Anticipation keen
My path had been selected
By a mighty hand unseen

Rebellious was my nature
Resisting every turn
Asleep at every lecture
Somehow I knew I'd learn

My path was not remembered
At least from what I knew
I had no love so tender
And honest men are few

My crooked path was jagged
The hills and mountains steep
My soul was somewhat ragged
My sorrow sometimes deep

My heart had been so battered
No one to care for me
My future seemed so shattered
My soul just could not see

So I turned my vision inward
A whole new world for me
The youth that was so wayward
Now smiled eternally

The weight of this world heavy
Was now transformed to light
And the water filled the levy
Oasis now in sight

The Craving

My soul had craved a better way
To greet the rising sun
Adventure in the way we play
Yet nothing left undone

A joyous love and energy
That captivates the heart
When chains are dropped and we are free
To finish what we start

Illusive changes, shifting tide
Yet steadfast in the soul
Direction guides us, path grows wide
And opens up the door

I asked the angels in the spheres
How best I could draw near
They answered, we are with you
Our voice inside you hear

And when you're drawing close to God
Your heavy heart will lift
And suddenly you feel so free
Your consciousness will shift

From a Distance

The moon appeared so round and smooth
Although a jagged rock
And we ourselves have peaks and grooves
And smooth the soul is not

But from a distance, from on high
We may appear half tame
But in the depths of inner soul
A lot of guilt and shame

And if the slate could be wiped clean
If we were born again
Would we choose a different path
Or would we be the same

If the Good Shepard heard your cry
Appeared beside your bed
And said this is the day you die
But he died then instead

Alone, without him, none could see
The way into the Light
And though we live we would be dead
And day would turn to night

The Treasure

I traveled in my dream last eve
It gave me second sight
I saw some things I can't believe
Revealed in the night

While cream will rise up to the top
But only when it's still
Our thoughts take wings and will not stop
No limits to His will

While sleeping in a quiet state
The mind will wander far
The soul remains yet wide awake
And reaching for the stars

Relax and float upon the wave
That rocks you fast asleep
And you will get all that you gave
But only love to keep

Your treasures soon will carry you
But you'll not carry them
For it is written all you do
You take with you, 'til then

No regret or judgment make
Nor burden any heart
Tis only time and love we take
The day we must depart

Gather not of treasures then
That must be left behind
But hold onto your every friend
Let love and kindness shine

Sow the good seed, share the love
For real love never dies
It's all we will take home with us
The day the spirit flies

The Manger

As baby in the manger lay
For a moment, it was I
Amid the soft and new mown hay
God's universe heard baby's cry

The mooing cows and baaing sheep
Proclaimed the child was born
And drifted into restful sleep
That magic Christmas morn

We've seen his star the wise men said
And followed it for days
We rejoice now and bring our gifts
And marvel in God's ways

The Magi were not mortal men
But sent from God on high
The gifts symbolic now as then
For newborns when they cry

These gifts and talents each receive
With guidance for our path
As Jesus said we must believe
And lean upon His staff

Thought

An ancient thought came 'round to me
Circumventing time
It nestled close where I could see
The rhythm of the rhyme

Original, nay, not one thought
They all have been before
A crescent wave born out at sea
Bounced from a distant shore

The thoughts we think are snapshots
On a roll of cosmic film
Developed in the darkness
Of how we really feel

The ones all framed and mounted
Are treasures that we've found
Manifesting proudly
From the mystic underground

Each thought is a negative
A frame on life's long roll
Each frame that we develop
A reflection of our soul

Hope mounted on the mantel
Love trapped behind a glass
If we need to get a reprint
All we have to do is ask

But when the reel is broken
The final frame has come
We return to write a movie
That has only just begun

And when the photo's faded
And the memories are lost
We rely upon the sages
To calculate the cost

Sparkling Earth

And when I gaze from earth to sky
Tis easy then to realize
A broadened heart and gladdened soul
And drink the beauty of the world

This planet precious in my eyes
And self inflicted all our cries
God's perfection on the earth
And out of pain we bring forth birth

In the twinkling of an eye
The floodgates open when we sigh
And with a deep and cleansing breath
Vibrations rise and mimic death

And from this vantage point we see
The mighty peaks and sparkling seas
Our life so small, expands so fast
And from this view we see at last

His form exquisite, glory bright
Enfolds us with His warming light
Love heals the soul, restores the sight
And lifts us out of darkest night

The Sprout

I reached across the abyss of time
A happy time when your soul touched mine
My heart was transformed to a holy shrine
Tears bitter like juice from a hand squeezed lime

My hand reaches out in the night for you still
My memory slides to the time you were ill
My heart reaches out with the sheer strength of will
My mind pushes back all the pain that I feel

My soul somehow knows of the sense it will make
When we realize God doesn't make a mistake
We never give more than we're willing to take
The seed cannot sprout until your heart breaks

God Sighed

I lay asleep and dreamed some dreams
And saw, not truth, but what it seems
I floated on the cosmic wave
So buoyantly, surreal and safe

I rode the ancient tidal swell
And met its lows in gates of hell
My soul rose with the rising tide
As if the breath of God had sighed

The steady rhythm brought me home
On tidal seas from where I roam
And underneath the sparkling sea
A trillion spirits helping me

The City

My soul washed up on the beach today
When sleep spit me out on the sand
I couldn't move, just couldn't get up
I could barely move a hand

My life had been in the sea last night
As I swam about in my dream
Recalling to mind the places I'd been
While flowing in spiritual streams

There is a river of which I've been told
Where angels and souls of men meet
Exchanging of love and thoughts that are grand
Where the love of God lights up the streets

And so far above in this gold light of love
Where the city glistens and shines
There is a house for each of us there
In a home made of Love Divine

Ignite the Spark

The building block that the builders forgot
Where the spirit lives and time it is not
Where the still waters run so quiet and deep
Where some are awake but most are asleep

Where the eternal moment is always now
Where the internal thought is written on brow
Here is the power that ignites the spark
Here is the flame that lights up the dark

Where energy spins in the space of a dot
Where matter doesn't matter and really is not
The atoms are made of pure energy
With the speed and the charge of electricity

As fluid and fast as the light from the sky
With every new question and every new why
Each heartbeat is sounded in rhythm and hum
With a hypnotic beat of a tribal drum

Guidance

I saw your face in midnight dreams
Your whispered thoughts were sunlight beams
My soul received your heartfelt smile
You lit a spark with your cool style

Cradled safe within your hand
My breathing comes with ease
I hear your voice across the land
Your whispers in the breeze

I'll let my mind be quiet, still
And let your light shine through
And you direct me where you will
This life I live for you

Instructions deep within my soul
Were planted long ago
A blueprint leading to the goal
To guide me then to bring me home

The Kingdom Is Within

Let thine eye be single on your goal
Seek the kingdom first we're told
Take up the cross and follow Him
Listen to the voice within

Words to live by Jesus said
Will heal your heart and clear your head
Learn again to be a child
He'll be with you all the while

Bless those who curse you, turn the cheek
You will find if you will seek
Only faith can make you whole
Only God can save your soul

Love your neighbor, judge him not
Thank the Lord for all we've got
If you've the faith of tiny seeds
The power of Love will fill your needs

Farewell Winter

The winter night so cold and still
With distant sounds of whippoorwill
With dreams of spring tucked in her wings
Vibrations of the earth she sings

When morning sun will warm the ground
And budding plants will hear the sound
And all of nature resurrects
The mighty trees and small insects

The humming, buzzing sounds of life
A great concerto day and night
The busy bee and butterfly
And graceful birds will ride the sky

The croaking frogs command the night
And all life sings with all their might
Good-bye bare winter welcome spring
And welcome all that warm air brings

Dream Clouds

I find a thought is like a cloud
A flowing, moving thing
That lifts our minds above the earth
On ethereal wings

A gathering of clouds a dream
Seen on the screen of sky
That dance and change in endless form
Responding as we sigh

The Valley of the Shadow

When the tunnel beckons me
I'll lift my eyes upward to see
The Light that says come onto me
Let go the body and fly free

My friends and loved ones gather near
I long to see their faces dear
I'll reach for you to guide me through
This valley of the shadow's view

This place we go when life is done
Where all our souls become as one
And we look down to those we love
Whose eyes don't see what's up above

Then swirling universe like tide
In the eddies, currents hide
And reach down like a whirlpool
And pull another from earth's school

Deep within the spiral funnel
Another soul is in the tunnel
Sanctioned by the One Who Knows
When best the time, the spirit grows

Upward with amazing speed
When the silver cord is freed
No longer bound to earthly clay
And none of us may know the day

So be prepared to meet the Host
Father, Son, and Holy Ghost
For now, full speed, you're coming home
To kneel before the Holy Throne

Hold On

The clock has ticked away the years
The fun times fly so fast
And with our laughter, also tears
But sad times never last

When countenance is fallen down
And broken heart still grieves
A smile will take away the frown
Of those who still believe

And healing, yes, will come in time
And stronger now we are
And He will help our soul to climb
At our appointed hour

Weeping may endure the night
So says the thirtieth psalm
But joy will come in morning light
He holds you safely in His palm

Spring

Seasons change and spring has sprung
The long cold days of winter, gone
The trees that stood so stark and bare
Now have blossoms for their hair

Downy are the tender leaves
Bursting forth to touch the breeze
Songbirds sing their serenade
Look at all that God has made

Beginnings

On the inward ear we hear
Tis joyous love that casts out fear
When we truly cast out fear
The angels guide and God will steer

Love heals, love heals
Love won't make deals
Love must be pure
Love must be real

And when the Master Potter calls
And claims the clay that's cracked and flawed
We, like the Genie in the lamp
Escape the pot that was our camp

For flesh cannot contain the soul
The spirit lives though flesh grows cold
And like Aladdin, God will say
I command your power this day

Grant me three things if you will
And I might adjust your bill
First, love the ones I dearly love
My creatures, plants, and stars above

The human souls your soul will touch
Treat them well and love them much
Next in service, teach them love
Spread the word that God above

Loves them each and every one
Every daughter, every son
Every creature in the sea
All the birds who fly the breeze

Every creature of the land
Is cradled in God's loving hand
Cherish them like God on high
For they, like us, do breathe and sigh

They feel the sun and love's embrace
No sparrow falls without a trace
That tiny spirit etched in time
A moment's flight in cosmic rhyme

And lastly rise and live for Me
Forsake all that you thought you'd be
And all of us be crucified
We start to live when we have died

Tapestry

Underneath this tapestry
The tangled knots and threads we see
Hidden from our earthly view
'Tis heaven's light makes all things new

This work of art viewed from above
Each thread unique and sewn with love
A new perspective heaven brings
When finally we have earned our wings

For every thread is quite precise
When viewed with heaven's loving eyes
But from below we only see
Appearance of disharmony

So keep the faith, the day will come
When heaven's sight will be your own
Appearances on earth deceive
'Til heaven's light persuades, Believe!

Awake This Fuzzy Morning

Awake this fuzzy morning
I open sleepy eyes
Still dreaming of you, darling
But then I realize

You left this world behind you
So many years ago
And now I cannot find you
Except when I'm alone

Without the world's distractions
I think about you still
I think about your actions
That finally got you killed

But most of all I think of love
And how it disappeared
Whatever were you thinking of
Those drug and booze filled years

I wish that you had reined it in
I prayed those habits gone
You were in a downward spin
In truth I was alone

I missed your lively spirit then
You tranquilized your mind
Although you were my closest friend
I left you far behind

I couldn't stay and watch you die
I had to leave you, dear
The booze-born rage would often fly
And freeze my heart with fear

Your spirit left your body then
Another soul stepped in
Your eyes would glaze with evil, friend
The demon was within

And though I helped you fight the fight
It wasn't quite enough
I had to leave that fateful night
When violence got too rough

To save myself I had to go
'Twas suicide to stay
But in my heart I'll always know
We'll meet again someday

Another life, another realm
Where love will stay and grow
And this time you will take the helm
And good seeds we will sow

Singing Wheels

In the silence of the space
Between the atoms feel
The music of the universe
Amidst the singing wheels

Magnetic force that holds the glue
Forever clinging power
Holds us with both grace and speed
And tracks both year and hour

Tipped in final balance act
The earth may spin and flip
And when we see destruction here
Tis not where spirit sits

We rise and fall and ride the wave
And in appointed time
It finally makes some sense to us
We live and never die

Did You?

Frozen dreary winter's day
Pendulum swings the other way
From summer's heat and warming sun
We feel old winter's work begun

We need more layers for the sheet
And need a way to warm our feet
The sun shines brightly far above
And here below we yearn for love

For two they say is best not one
To lift us up to find the sun
And when, at last, we find a friend
He may not stay to journey's end

For heaven calls her soldiers home
And decorates them from the throne
Who did you help, protect and serve
When others may have lost their nerve

And did you hear the hungry call
And did you ever give your all
And in the midst of battle ground
Could you still hear the trumpet sound

And when you pray, do you look up
When overflowing was your cup
And say I'm thankful for this day
Or did you look the other way

And did you say Praise be to God
Before they cover you in sod
And did you comfort those who mourn
And lend your coat in winter's storm

And from your warm bed, did you rise
And meet the day with hopeful eyes
And ask who may I bless this day
To send some comfort out their way

Who Are We?

In the crystal ball I see
A glimpse of all eternity
Exploding stars and cosmic wind
The messengers that God will send

Eyes so bright and warm and wise
Wink at me from sun bleached skies
Answers come when questions flow
And all our lives we strive to know

The greatest mysteries known to God
Who are we? Why do we plod
Upon this plane, this mother earth
Toward life and death, another birth

What is this place where we were born
Can fools like us not ever learn
So guide my life, do what You will
Take this vessel, peace be still

Fill it with eternal flame
The Holy Ghost in Jesus's name
The angels hear our human song
And joy wells up and love is strong

Star Shine

Deep within the cosmic mind
The stars and lovely planets shine
Their light and love has traveled far
Reveals to us the distant star

And we emit a sparkle too
A light that brightens me and you
Like solitary stars that shine
This living light is yours and mine

And though a distant star may die
Its light lives on and meets the eye
Forever with the speed of light
The star shines on to light the night

Never fading, never gone
We, like stars, shine on and on
The Maker lit our hearts with love
And shines within and shines above

The Vow

If love could wait, the passion hold
I'd still be trapped in marriage cold
But what you gave was not so real
You never seemed to deeply feel

My love was lost on you, my dear
And now another holds me near
And all my life I wondered how
A man or wife could break their vow

You gave to me such worldly things
And most of all my wedding ring
From deep inside you didn't give
Tis just a show the way we live

And now my heart longs to be free
I cast my fate to destiny
I am a prisoner in our home
I must break free, with pain I groan

The luster of this life has gone
Within this house I am alone
Another soul has searched for me
And found me clinging desperately

To what was once a wedding vow
But now seems lost and sad somehow
How did we get here to this place
How can we leave with no disgrace

Would Jesus ever sanction this
If we did part with one last kiss
Alone, though tethered, two souls now
Who once upon a time did vow

My love for you was once so strong
No longer can I tag along
My soul in pain, with groans I cry
Tears streaming down with eyes to sky

My heart may burst if I stay here
And up ahead my path is clear
Forsake all others we once said
But now my heart feels cold and dead

Is this the way tis meant to be
My hating you, you hating me
The child we made with God's good care
Now watches sadly from the stair

Thoughts Take Wings

Swifter than the speed of light
The speed of thought created types
The type of images we made
Produced by thoughts of sun and shade

Thoughts born of love and born of hate
These images became our fate
Thinking strength and thinking fear
We manifest what we hold dear

Clinging to our basic thoughts
Think clearly on the good we've got
Weed out the thoughts that poison mind
Focus on the thoughts that shine

For we see darkly through the glass
Our visions manifest, then pass
Plant another Godly seed
To take the place of wild weed

Dwell on the good and lovely things
For truly do our thoughts take wings
And with a bit of leaven rise
Heartfelt thoughts will crystallize

An Instrument of Love

Upon an empty canvas here
I write some words to rhyme
My mind a blank, my cat so near
At last, some idle time

A time to think and gather in
The purpose held in life
A chance to ask directions now
And filter out all strife

Reflections all bounce back to me
Upon my vacant mind
And images all dance and weave
A tapestry divine

But seek I now to know the thread
My Lord would have me weave
The dreams that dance inside my head
And teach me to believe

Are but an instrument of love
To teach while we're asleep
Shone down from heaven up above
Are promises to keep

This light invades the waiting heart
And then illumines mind
From this light we never part
And love will seek His kind

And take this time in daily thought
And listen with the heart
And you will find what you have sought
The rest will God impart

Night Visits

I see you in my dreams at night
Your luminescent soul
And there I hold you, oh so tight
Your heart in mine I hold

And often when I travel there
You speak of things to come
And help me with my every fear
And keep my spirit young

I reach to you across the veil
You hand entwines with mine
With your love, I cannot fail
Our mission is divine

Listen

Listen to the silences
Between the atom's dance
The God-space that creates
All of happenstance

Here the song is written
Here the angels dwell
Here the alpha concept
Of a heaven or a hell

Drink and breathe the ether
Of this potent, quiet space
Where fairies and ghosts linger
Where God made your tiny face

The Lighthouse

As I slept my soul was kept
From leaving earth behind
And gingerly I took each step
Escaping just my mind

Returning now I saw that how
We live from day to night
Enriches all within our brow
And turns from wrong to right

Reflecting here on earthly plane
We gaze within the soul
And measure all we lose and gain
All fragments of the whole

And melting into God at night
We leave our earthly home
Embracing all in nightly flight
As through the sky we roam

And with the twinkling of a star
We're guided on the path
And know that God is near, not far
He rises when we laugh

The joy of the heart is real
As we connect to Him
And no one can this joy steal
This joy has no end

Though sorrows come and sorrows go
Like darkness in the light
Brilliant light will stop the woe
And light the darkest night

And woe be gone, the light we see
Is from the Maker's hand
He lights the sky and earth and tree
The ocean and the land

And like a mighty lighthouse beam
He leads his children home
For all is not quite what it seems
All clay and dust and foam

The spirit dwells between the spheres
That spin and whirl and groan
And all we see, taste, touch, and hear
Reflect from heaven's home

Love Now

Below the clouded shrouded sun
My mind surveyed the work I'd done
And through the gentle morning mist
I saw the souls of all I'd kissed

What had I done on Mother Earth
To give myself a sense of worth
Who had I loved and let them know
A hundred, nay, a thousand more

To greet each other with a kiss
A chance the heart must never miss
How long we're here, how long we play
And none of us will know the day

When this life on earth is done
Ask did we work and have some fun
Is our mission now complete
And may we kiss the Master's feet

Children of the planet earth
Your life does not begin with birth
Your soul lives on and seeks to know
The arrows from the Master's bow

Atom and Eve

If we think of thoughts that flow
As iridescent things
The thought expands and flowers grow
The thought has taken wings

A thought can form a molecule
Or tear one up it seems
The universe we look upon
Is built by many dreams

There is no end to dreaming
Or seeking 'til we find
And life's a mighty mystery
To which we have been blind

Within this inner sanctum
We hear the atom's song
As they whiz about with fever
We're compelled to sing along

And in this holy corridor
We meet the angels there
They're living all around us
In what we call thin air

Come Back

Each time he healed, he said, "Go and sin no more
Your faith hath made thee whole"
And when you knock in seeking your path
I will open the door

Wasn't it said Elias must come
Before men would see the Messiah, the Son
He had already come but men knew him not
Elias was John who was killed in a plot

The head on the platter was that of a man
Whose number was up in the hourglass of sand
But mansions are many in our Father's home
The body's our temple while on earth we roam

Elias has come and gone many times
A spirit of leaven to raise human minds
We entertain angels oft unaware
Who guide us away from the tempter's snare

And though a man's name be Elias or John
Or a woman's is Mary, or Sarah, or Joan
The Spirit will fly away to our God
Though the body be covered with six feet of sod

The spirit returns for the next job to do
Housed in a body so tiny and new
Truly a miracle mansion of clay
To house an old soul for its next brief stay

Rejoice

This is the day which the Lord hath made
Let us rejoice and be glad
Open your ears to the bird's serenade
Think on the lovely, not bad

Armed with the truth that strengthens me
I can accomplish all things
This is the truth that sets us free
And living it earns us our wings

'Tis truth that Christ preached to love and forgive
Makes our burdens both easy and light
He taught us to know our Father wants us to live
And to love with all of our might

The Maker's Plan

You are my friend, I've loved you from
The moment we were born
Not birth on earth, but long before
The planet earth was formed

Yes, you and I were standing there
And saw our Maker's face
Our souls like snowflakes floating through
The deepest, darkest space

Propelled through space
The Maker's breath gently sent us on
A loving journey meeting friends
Upon our earthly home

When I see you, I will know
Your beauty and your grace
And looking straight into your eyes
Will see our Maker's face

For you and I are but the same
Of love's pure energy
The light within we share with God
We breathe in harmony

The breath of life He gave to us
Put blueprints in our hearts
And if you ask, you will receive
The gifts that Love imparts

And when our earthly task's complete
He calls the snowflakes home
Angels come to meet and greet
And bring us to His throne

Ultimately, He does know
Each snowflake by its name
Every detail, every thought
Of every snowflake frame

Each heart within the flakes will melt
To feel the Maker's love
And journey out again in time
On wings sent from above

Memory of Battle

The blood that once was splattered here
Still shines a crimson red
The rage that spent itself in fear
Now waits with certain dread

The fear that raged in battle, dear
Still plays within your head
And though it's quiet for a while
It's never really dead

Our House

Our house, atomic energy
A tent where spirit dwells
The ethers freely roam about
Through paper thin atomic walls

 Tiny pillars shaped by mind
Are thinly wrapped and veiled
Atoms whirl and find their kind
And leave the comet's trail

Molecules are towered high
Vibrating in their dance
Vast space to spare and love to share
But nothing done by chance

Thin Air

Shimmering teardrops make me see
Through crystal lids that shaded me
A new dimension gaining ground
Beyond the earthly sights and sounds

So intimate within the heart
A brand new world and brand new start
Arising from the knees in prayer
Arising from what is called thin air

A teeming lively spirit world
Kundalini sleeps uncoiled
Awaken to the earth and sun
To live and love and venture on

The Tree

Wide awake on Christmas morn
I gazed upon the stars
Each tiny light upon the tree
Sparkling angel harps

The tree itself unique each year
The symbol of our lives
Decorated, disappears
With beauty in its life

Each new season, each new tree
Has glory 'til it dies
Much like this fleeting life we see
That fades before our eyes

This glory in our moment now
We seize upon this day
And all the dreams within our brow
Will surely come our way

So lift your dreams and sanctify
We've quite a duty here
To glorify the One on high
Let Him take your ship to steer

World Without End

I looked into my crystal ball
And marveled at the things I saw
Unfolding drama without end
Parents, lovers, pets and friends

The script was written long ago
And practiced in another show
Each line and dance and every song
Is fitted to the path we're on

Our joy and woe placed carefully
Our tears and fears will shake our tree
And in the storm our limbs will bend
Unfolding world without end

Be of Good Cheer

Unassuming, unimagined
Spirit guides along the way
Whisper softly to our hearts
For soon will come a brighter day

All that confronts us and astounds us
Soon will be part of darker days
How much longer, fears grow stronger
Soul uplifts us, spirit shifts us
Don't lose heart, God lights the way

Mercy tender, we surrender
Grant us strength just for today
Joy uplifts us, love will shift us
Beauty, peace will come to stay

Guidance

He has helped us mark the way
Prepared us for another day
Given us good gifts that last
And guidance if we would but ask

Learn from what the spirit says
The still small voice within the head
The gifts we bring beyond the grave
Are gifts of spirit that we gave

A simple smile along the way
That brightens someone else's day
A tone of kindness in the voice
A thought to make a righteous choice

A helping hand to lift a load
A gentle push along the road
The time to hear another's dream
A stitch or two to mend a seam

A hug to say I'm here for you
The love that binds like spirit glue
Courage in the face of fear
Triumphs in the sojourn here

Bring sunshine on a rainy day
And stay the course, come what may
A true heart for all those you love
And seeking guidance from above

Encouragement to those in need
Lending strength to those that grieve
Sympathy to those in pain
All of these are spirit gains

For we as spirit seek this earth
And choose to have this earthly birth
Immortal spirit all are we
And cling to life tenaciously

Crunchy Little Chips of Sky

Crunchy little chips of sky
I grabbed them as they floated by
I held their essence in my palm
Just long enough to sing along

What great treasure touched me then
A loving thought from long lost friend
In the ether you are now
And yet you speak to me somehow

Our hearts once met on earthly plane
And now you're here with me again
What secrets do you share with me
Til I like you will soon fly free

What writing on akashic scroll
Will light the path on earth below
What say the prophets of the age
What magic might the soul engage

What light beneath the bushel shines
We need new vessels for new wine
What be our duties as we live
But only for our love to give

The moon so pale yet so bold
Reflects the light of stories told
Some say we live some say we die
Some say we're blessed by God on high

But choose this day your daily bread
And gather good seed for your head
And grab those little chips of sky
And rise to meet them as they fly

Patience

Deep within her patience
She caused the days to change
For the sad heart and the faithless
She was clearly out of range

Her rays shined down upon us
Like water on the grass
We soaked in all her luster
As her hours slowly passed

Reflecting on the Father
Light when day is done
We bowed our heads in wonder
Saved by love, His only son

In the darkness grew the first roots
Then the light that drew us up
Like a magnet for the first shoots
Then we shared the Master's cup

With the clock of heaven spinning
And the sands in hourglass
We wonder if we're winning
As our darkest moments pass

If we tune into the cosmos
And listen for a star
We just may hear the burning
And the churning where we are

In the coolness of the faces
Of ever changing moon
We still may see the traces
Of the past and future soon

But only with the patience
And the ups and downs of Job
With the eye of hope not faithless
May we wear the purple robe

From the River

Out of thin air and buoyant on the water
Is a thought form like a bird who is playful as an otter
They oft times go unnoticed as they race across the mind
But their messages will linger as they float on salt and brine

Be still beside the river as you meditate and pray
Cast your bread unto the fishes lest they turn and swim away
Surrender all the worry you have chosen to embrace
Peace be still and listen for the coming of His grace

Majestic Hymn

Majestic hymn within the mind
Hums the sound of God divine
The music captures deep the soul
Wounds are healed and we're made whole

No words nor drugs nor surgery
But magic in the way we see
To know but only truth and love
Will heal the soul by God above

Love will light the darkest space
And truth will light the saddest face
And when this light shines from within
Will warm the soul and joy we win

Oh, outer careless fearful world
Our faith and love is now our sword
The dragons of this world obey
The Son of God who guides the way

Immortal love we know you now
You slay the beast within somehow
You right the thought that is our crown
And now we float no longer drown

The tempest, though, be strong and fierce
It cannot this new armor pierce
The holy breath has cleansed us well
No longer bound to earthly shell

Now floating in the ocean foam
The earthly yoke from us is torn
No struggle now no need to fight
We rise to the eternal light

The war is finished we are new
From higher realms and higher view
The dark has lifted mind is bright
And now we see we're made of light

All sons and daughters bound to God
And looking back on earth we trod
Among the many still asleep
Yet all the light and love we keep

Every moment all is love
All manifest by God above
And here below we overflow
No need to strive and still we grow

Like flower faces chasing sun
Or children's prayers when day is done
Each stitch upon this life we weave
Then double stitch we do not leave

Coal to Diamonds

In the early morning light
My soul breathes in your soul
With half closed eyes we clearly see
The diamond in the coal

I'll make a diamond from the coal
You left inside my heart
The ashes from the dreams you stole
Will rise and spark the dark

Another day, another love
Will soon be on the rise
For there is guidance from above
Another set of eyes

He sees the tears and sees the lies
That blur your broken dreams
He'll lift you to much bluer skies
For all's not what it seems

The seeds were scattered long ago
With strong and loving hand
He goes with you where e're you go
Upon the shifting sand

He cradles you and sees your thoughts
And helps them to expand
And reaches with precision
To lend a helping hand

And if you listen you may hear
A voice call out to you
The mist will rise your path is clear
In all things that you do

The Gift

In the haze of sleepy mind
We search the dreams and then we find
A distant shadow brought to light
A form invisible by night

A ghostly spirit in my head
Transformed as I lay on my bed
A friendly sort an angel dear
Assures me and I have no fear

I'll walk with you a little while
Reflecting love I feel your smile
As sun burns off the thinning haze
I'm thankful for these peaceful days

The journey long and sometimes steep
We cling to love for that we keep
And through our dreams we nourish life
And fan the flame that gives us light

A misty cloud-like thought appears
And cools the sun or rains down tears
And quickly on the screen of mind
They disappear but leave behind

An image that was quickly caught
Impressed the ether with that thought
And in the dark room brought to light
A sacred gift called second sight

The House

Once upon a time there was a house upon the land
Nestled in the rocks where the ocean meets the sand
The house withstood the weather in the sunshine and the rain
When the waves could go no higher and the wind howled like a train

And love lit up the house and made a cozy home
And love had placed each brick each rafter and each stone
And love had promised always to keep in good repair
To maintain the very structure as long as love is there

The foundation very solid and the roof is a great shield
The windows gather light in but the walls will never yield
As long as love has built it as long as love endures
As long as love is welcome within these mighty doors

As long as there is starlight by day the shining sun
As long as love will lift us the day has just begun
As the Mighty Spirit leads us and guides us by the hand
May our footsteps always take us where the ocean meets the sand

Tis Love That Spins the Planets

From the brink of heartbreak
Of sadness and despair
The clouds for me had parted
When I saw you standing there

The joy of heaven opened
Like the sunshine on the rain
Gone was all the heartache
As I held you once again

Time had lost her memory
Space did not exist
Yet here we were together
Where time and space had kissed

The moments that we treasure
All melded up in one
Where lightning shot her arrow
Into the rising of the sun

The memory and the magic
That ignited in the sky
Had rippled through the universe
Blessed by God on high

And angel wings embrace us
And lift us when we fall
Tis love that spins the planets
And love that binds us all

The Hour Glass

Drifting image screen of mind
I watch you flow and ebb
Reaching deep within I find
An echo of the words we said

Lingering in silent stream
Suspended in the flow
The beauty of a longed for dream
And pain to watch it go

Our thoughts like threads will twist and knot
And bind another near
We take for granted all we've got
Then watch it disappear

We ask the help of guiding force
To shape this thing called Mind
Assist us as we make a choice
For if we seek we find

Lifted up a sacred vow
Had captured deep my soul
The past and future present now
Unrolling holy scroll

The blueprint from a master plan
Now smudged with fallen tears
The hourglass has lost its sand
And come to end of years

The earth gives up her misty dead
Released to fly the stars
But leaves behind a sense of dread
And wonders where you are

Many Flights

Like a falling wounded bird
I give my soul to you
Grateful for the many flights
And sunsets that I knew

Willingly I give up now
Surrender weary bones
The final flight from this lifetime
Will bring me to my home

And there the spirit waters wash
Refresh my weary soul
Baptizing with a cleansing bath
To reach the other shore

Another world another place
Another space in time
Where love will meet and we will know
Of innocence divine

For this is where He leadeth me
Beside the water still
By greenest pastures, bluest skies
Through effort of His will

And I will follow seeds of faith
He's planted in my heart
And though the slings and arrows sting
From Him I won't depart

Remembering

In the effervescent dawn
As the sun began to rise
Came the lifting of the fog
And a dazzling to the eyes

The colors were so brilliant
With the coming of the day
And life seemed so resilient
As the sunshine spread his rays

But the night was not quite over
There were many more to come
With the turning of the stars and moon
And spinning of the sun

We get to glimpse a mystery
Of which we are a part
Not written down in history
But written on the heart

That inner star is rising
That connects you to the rest
This may not be surprising
As you follow inner quest

But what Pandora's Box is open
That alas we cannot seal
Is it words that we have spoken
Or wounds we cannot heal

Every thought that we selected
Each act we chose to do
Each talent we perfected
Each sigh and breath we drew

It all will be remembered
In a season of due time
Now lying in the chambers
Of the heart and of the mind

Take Heart

Upon the open plain I saw
Man put to rest and nothing more
No choir song or epitaph
This king had finally breathed his last

The loyal subjects bowed down now
And sanctified his life somehow
Though cruel and vicious he had been
He ruled the land, but that was then

And now he laid his body down
Gave up the ghost gave up his crown
The pages of his time had turned
On funeral pyre he was burned

And all his people now were free
From cruel and tortured legacy
Their leader gone they scattered far
Not knowing who or what they are

They look to whom they cannot find
Their star within they left behind
They seek it now on yonder hill
Illusive goal they wander still

The compass deep within the breast
Had long since slept at man's request
They followed rulers like lost sheep
Their inner star still fast asleep

Awaken now and follow not
The cruel king in his rule forgot
The frightened people need to pray
And look at life another way

Be still the heart be still the mind
And never leave your soul behind
Follow not an evil man
Though so attractive is his plan

For God alone can make you whole
And heal the body heal the soul
Look to another never friend
For God is with you to the end

And never is the end you see
For you will rise with destiny
A son-ship with the Holy One
When journey on this earth is done

And set your sail to fly with Him
No other guide no other King
And focus not on earthly kings
Nor treasures of the earthly things

But focus like the laser beam
For all is not just what it seems
Of Truth and Love we are a part
Of single mind and single heart

Deja Vu

If anyone could see through space
And wonder at the sky
And find a life that lives through grace
And without wings can fly

We know that we have been there
We know we've lived before
Remember what we've seen here
And crossed that open door

The memory still lingers
The heart still sings that song
The sound of many singers
As we all sing along

And with one ear we listen
And with one voice we sing
And morning dew will glisten
As it feels the sunshine sting

And as the vapor rises
We ask where it will go
And will there be surprises
On high or here below

Light Cleanse

Sometimes sit I by myself
Wondering about all things
I must not sit upon a shelf
Or like a bell I cannot ring

Move about and follow dreams
Let Spirit be the guide
For all is not just what it seems
And after life we do not die

Precision clock the moon and sun
Precise the earth and tide
A wonder all that God has done
The miracle of life

From birth to death and back again
A resurrection sure
Strive to touch the hem of Him
Through whom all life endures

As sunlight penetrates the cloud
And finds its way to earth
So the Lord will lift the shroud
Revealing all our worth

Our temple lit by heavens light
Will open wide the doors
The midday sun replaces night
And sunshine will endure

The windows of the soul still shut
Will crack and open wide
And love will move the bolt and nut
That locks us deep inside

The corners of the house now lit
Swept clean by cleansing sun
Will not return to dirt and grit
For error's been undone

Mercy Now

The dove a symbol of new life
A symbol of deep peace
Returning with an olive leaf
New hope of calmer seas

The eagle proud so brave and strong
A king of earth and air
So clear of eye his vision great
A brother that we share

For we are one both great and small
So intertwined are we
And when we touch the web of life
Tis felt on land and sea

The wind may rage the rain may pour
The mountains may erupt
But how we handle all of these
Is how we drink our cup

And creatures are not less than we
Though some at our command
The good Lord God created these
With loving brilliant hand

With mercy tend the garden here
For mercy take a stand
Transform the stoney heart within
Let love now rule the land

Entertaining angels with
A kindness in the heart
No slaughter of the innocence
Let good and evil part

A new day now is dawning
Burnt sacrifice now gone
For God is Love and Love is God
More beauty from now on

No arrogance but meekest pride
As man is born again
Perspective changed and now we see
The creatures as our friend

Light the Corners

If only evil was known to be
The absence only of good
This from the knowledge this from the tree
And clearly be understood

We then see the dark as it truly is
Merely the absence of light
A shadow unmasked that thinks it has hid
Though the nights overcome by the light

In the deepest of corners of mortal mind
In the dark places of the soul
Lies a hope that the light will finally find
All the corners and darkness will go

The Song

I feel the breath of angel wings
Stirring round my heart
Whispering of brand new things
Of which I am a part

A voice in silence calls to me
A magnet to my ear
Assures me that He cradles me
And that He's always near

In trouble and in joyful times
He never leaves my side
And lifts me up so buoyantly
Amid the rushing tide

Open up that inner ear
Where sings that inner song
Where once we simply could not hear
But now we sing along

The rising sun had just begun
To wake up sleepy eyes
The stars appeared to fade away
Retreat from colored skies

As earth warmed up the seas and trees
And clouds formed little thoughts
My inner soul was still at ease
My mind was fraught with naught

There rose upon a crest of wave
An image of your face
My heart embraced the love you gave
So full of hope and grace

My love encircles you, my friend
A blessing that I wear
A circle that can have no end
A bubble that we share

So fortunate at last we see
What always has been there
The crest of wave has risen high
And lifted love so rare

The Journey

In the beauty of your smile
I hope you know deep love
And fashioned in the Lord's own style
Wrapped in light from up above

And on your journey may this light
Your inner sanctum fill
And may He give you second sight
Good judgment in free will

And may you always search your soul
In choices that you make
Keep love and God your single goal
And give more than you take

And may you rise to meet the trials
That will surely come your way
And may you love the many miles
As you journey through your days

Transition

The morning sun was rising high
The daylight moon grew dim
The stars had faded from the sky
The birds all chirped their hymn

Seemed time was flying faster now
Days soon turned into years
Wolves still looked to moon to howl
And rain clouds still shed tears

And time, illusive abstract thing
That measures moves through space
Can it measure angels' wings
Or trace the lines on wrinkled face

And do these lines wrap our cocoon
And someday we emerge
A butterfly from lowly worm
When time and space will merge

Angels' Alley

A peaceful sound within the sky
Can oftentimes be heard
A band of angels flitting by
Or was that just a bird

An angel's breath can stir the breeze
And cause the mist to rise
And fly upon the storm with ease
Then clear the darkened skies

A whispered prayer within the heart
Can stir the mist again
Our tears can stir the rain to start
Then cause the rain to end

And ancient sun we feel your power
Nourishing our earth
Synchronizing every hour
Celebrating every birth

And in the dim and gentle light
Of waning crescent moon
Were tracers of the angels' flight
Dispelling thoughts of gloom

Mystified still half asleep
Reflecting on a dream
I left a place called "Angels' Alley"
Swept away by rushing stream

Here my spirit went to school
To learn of things unseen
Here the Master Golden Rule
Is principal and dean

We learned about the great "I am"
From prophets gone before
And learned that all we think we can
We'll do and even more

Earth Battle

The silky mist that hugged the sky
Reflected sadness in my eyes
A thousand soldiers daily fell
A thousand letters home to tell

Of courage in a war of hell
A passage rung on steeple bell
Etched in time repeated stage
Theater of immoral rage

Each side determined they are right
To enter fierce and mighty fight
To slay the dragon, kill the wrong
In glory sounding battle song

And who's in charge when we all die
And who will sound the battle cry
We pass the torch to children's hands
Who still are crawling soon to stand

And with the torch we pass the fears
And hatred of a thousand years
For when was time when war was not
Eternal earthly battles fought

Beginnings

The moonlit bay returned my gaze
Reminded me of brighter days
Reflected in this soul of mine
The days of honey, milk, and wine

A countenance with chin held up
The Master there who passed the cup
A sip of this I dare not drink
Without His touch to make me think

The world a strange and lonely place
Without His strength we cannot face
The trials and terrors, many here
Yet in His presence, have no fear

A joy so full and love complete
When I am by the Master's feet
Forgot not we belong to Him
With all our woes and all our sin

And tears we cry are not in vain
But nourish souls with heaven's rain
And when our spirits fly the skies
We'll see ourselves through heaven's eyes

No longer bound to dust and clay
The seeds we planted sprout today
And gently warmed up by the sun
Our real life's work has just begun

Hello Again

I loved you once and you loved me
A thousand years ago
Another world another sea
Another distant shore

I dreamed of you then sealed that song
And locked it in my heart
Not knowing how my soul would long
For what was torn apart

Long distant days and summer haze
Had clouded my clear eyes
I couldn't meet the steady gaze
Of stars in clear night skies

My broken soul was still in pain
And writhed in mortal fear
My bright full moon set now to wane
A new star rose to steer

Now homeward bound my soul found rest
My journey near an end
This vessel creaking and still stressed
Had found a long lost friend

With comfort now but tears to spill
We cling to what is left
And though our love had lost its thrill
We think it for the best

With now our feet on solid ground
We journey down the hill
And from this view we look around
To lusher valleys still

Illusions

In a castle, ancient, deep
I wandered in its bowels
My spirit up but still asleep
Was lost for what seemed hours

My only guide, an inner voice
That told me I must rise
That in this life we make a choice
To see the truth through lies

For what seems true may sometimes be
A blatant lie at best
And sometimes what we think we see
Is east disguised as west

And what rings true within the heart
Will strike that long lost chord
And this may be the very start
To free the stone from sword

The magic that can loose the spell
Illusions that we see
Will shake the earth we knew so well
And shake us til we're free

In Spite Of

You lead me to a bitter stream
Where fallen angels dwell
Your love was false, destroyed the dream
And brought me close to hell

 I drank the cup you gave to me
Not knowing it was rank
My trust misplaced now plain to see
My heart within me sank

But love betrayed in many ways
Still searches for the light
Still longing for the brighter days
Escaping darkest night

Like Flowers

And though much kinder we could be
While pilgrims in this world
A greater power oversees
Our deeds and all our words

With tender mercy we are judged
While searching for the light
We grow in dirty fertile fields
Not knowing left from right

But hope remains and faith will grow
To light the darkness here
Like flowers reaching for the sun
We rise above this sphere

In Due Season

The days have flown they rightly say
Like autumn leaves have blown away
Like once in spring their promise came
And life was full with summer rain

The winter blast will soon blow through
Erase, prepare for something new
The world will spin and stars will rise
We'll still look up to sparkling skies

And when our days are done at last
And dry like leaves from summers past
Our hearts within prepare for spring
As winter sweeps the cold floor clean

Mystified

So mystified my mind was now
To know You saw and heard somehow
You feel my joy and feel my pain
You know my loss and know my gain

Your ever present love it seems
Is in my soul and in my dreams
And never do I go too far
That You don't light my shining star

And ever when I close my eyes
I see Your rainbow in my skies
You comfort me I overflow
And now my heart will always know

That where I go You also go
And who I am You also know
You are within and by my side
My ever present loving guide

And when my compass points to north
Another miracle will come forth
Another day to sing Your praise
Another way You bless my days

And always in my time of need
Your angels sow the healing seed
And time unfolds the harvest here
The angels whisper they are near

The Message

Through the glass darkly your image appeared
And then in a flash became crystal clear
I saw in that moment all that I need
To look in your soul, your heart I could read

Your image was that of a man royal blue
You stood tall and took pride in all that you do
The love of your family still sung in your heart
Confusion and sadness of why you're apart

Your energy strummed on your untouched guitar
And played the clean notes of your chart in the stars
A message came through for your wife and your son
Please tell her you're here and that life does go on

The Journey

I rest my mind in nature's arms
Suspended from the stars
Planted here and safe from harm
Between Venus and Mars

A likely place to land this craft
Within the Milky Way
My joy is great and I must laugh
And yes I plan to stay

The journey never really ends
Although we've traveled far
We join with others we call friends
To find our own bright star

From east to west I turn my bow
To face the setting sun
The midday noontide far behind
My work here almost done

The minutes tick the years fly by
We greet another day
The times we laughed and times we cried
Will never really stay

A fleeting thing this life we have
As time she marches on
The sun will rise on other days
But this one is well done

Farewell, my life, farewell, my friends
I've loved you and I've learned
That friendship never really ends
And seasons always turn

From Mary

My virgin son, I send you forth
A lamb among the wolves
I loved you well before your birth
Before this earthly world

Your name of love will render still
The darkest evil force
And lovingly, we bow to Thee
And sing in grateful voice

My son, I loved you with full heart
Before the world began
And all of nature knows your chart
You are the great "I AM"

In quiet stillness of my prayer
I sense you here with me
And always I can feel you there
My heart has eyes to see

In tearful, grateful earthly sigh
My soul will breathe you in
And all of nature does reply
There's room at every inn

My Brother

Next time you journey to this place
We'll plan to visit more
And now I may not see your face
You're bound for distant shores

Next time you said I'd see you here
You'd stay a little longer
Next time we'd toast a wine or beer
But now you must grow stronger

Next time you plan tomorrow's trip
Tomorrow never comes
The Lord cannot just hold that ship
While we go have our fun

The Lord, He has a different plan
And now your ship must sail
So we will love you while we can
The love that cannot fail

This timeless trip, who knows the time
When we'll be called back home
I feel the family gather now
You will not be alone

Though strength is failing on this side
It grows beyond the veil
And heaven's door will open wide
And through this gate you'll sail

And one day not too distant now
Our names will be called too
Before the King we all must bow
We'll gather next to you

You've been my brother and my friend
On earth for all my years
You know this story never ends
And brings forth joy and tears

Our Mother Earth and Father Son
Has blessed our journey here
And now your new life has begun
The dance among the spheres

And when a leaf shall wave to me
Or Spirit breezes by
I'll think of you and how you're free
And see you in a while

Atom

My frozen heart now strangely still
Escapes the task to do God's will
Somehow we know what's wrong and right
And yet return from day to night

The angel dark has spread his wings
But still the God within him sings
It's not too late to seek the light
For God gives all an inner sight

He guides our steps, He knows our fears
And all our changes through the years
And in the vacuum of deep space
Is where we dare to seek his face

He dwells between each atom here
So silent still so very near
Within, without His hold is strong
Between the whirring atoms' calm

For Heaven's Sake

The clock ticks on but won't tick back
Until we mourn and wear our black
When comes the end we see the first
And fate decides which one is worse

Did we lose or did we gain
Each day a link upon the chain
And in the end will we be strong
Will heaven sing a victory song

And all we give and all we take
We bring with us for heaven's sake
And all the deeds we left undone
And all the songs we've never sung

We take the seeds of all we are
Contained within our shining star
And mercy shakes to separate
The loving seeds from those of hate

And pours His Holy Spirit down
And penetrates the chakra crown
Now wheels in motion we can see
The meaning of our history

And now full circle we must face
Was it grace or just disgrace
No hiding now, our secrets known
The images are now full blown

This is the judgment at the end
We see ourselves as foe or friend
Though we've been blind we realize
The meaning of our sighs and cries

And all the love we give and take
Returns to us for heaven's sake
And all that fills our heart and soul
Is what we reap and what we sow

I Thirst

Pondering life and death as one
I thought of mighty streams
That flow until the journey's done
I found, or so it seems

The ocean body welcoming
The stream from whence it came
It's really a beginning
This giant mass of rain

The river thought its end was near
While rushing to the sea
But now its fate is crystal clear
Its spirit now is free

Good Night

The sleepy moon all clothed in white
Suspended in the sky
Decorates the starry night
As earthly lovers sigh

Oh beautiful celestial orb
How much you must have seen
Hearts and bodies loved and torn
Nightly on the earthly scene

To view the moon and see your face
So tenderly I see
Your tears and laughter left its trace
Reflecting back to me

Our Mother Earth has gathered near
The spirits of the skies
And of the land and sea we hear
Our Mother groans and cries

Our Father holds the balance now
And bathes in brilliant light
That burns and cleanses as we bow
Our heads to say good night

Wander Dreams

The light of the sun came creeping in
The dawn of early morn
My soul gave flight to reach the house
Into which I was born

We wander far in nightly treks
Though some remember not
This knowledge that we're not at home
Begot the vampire lot

But as we travel in our dreams
Not all is lost at dawn
Impressions in the mind, like clouds
Will ripen and move on

Refreshing rain to cleanse the mind
And shaping crystal streams
Defying laws of space and time
Creating healing springs

Angels, they will lift you up
And guide you in the way
As you share the Master's cup
We drink both night and day

The Spell

Here in this empty space I dwell
Time no longer I can tell
My fate is not cast to the wind
I fly on all the thoughts I send

I fly between the alpha waves
And ride the crest from birth to grave
And parting is so bittersweet
We kiss and cry and then retreat

And somewhere sounds the warning bell
Synchronized to break the spell
A misty, mystic moment shared
Then magically the soul's propelled

Behind the veil my spirit peeked
And saw the souls so long asleep
Amid the dreams of other realms
I heard the music of the bells

A tinkling first, but then full blown
The sound that calls the children home
Like many candles in the dark
I saw within each soul a spark

Some brighter now, some growing dim
But each a light, a gift from Him
And none were hid beneath the shade
But all were lights that God has made

The Prison

I peered from in my prison dark
Craving warmth of sun
No light for me, internal spark
My life had come undone

The blueprint of my life was lost
My feet had lost the path
Such grief and sorrow this has caused
Full circle come at last

So upward swam I toward the sky
And peace my body filled
My mind had ceased to ask Him why
My fears and qualms were stilled

The reins I handed o'er to Him
Control had disappeared
He wiped my brow, forgave my sin
And now I let Him steer

My prison gone, I see the sun
That warms so deep my soul
A sacred journey has begun
This tiny bud unfolds

The Peak

In the lazy stream of mind
I rode the river there
No sense of space, no sense of time
So far away from here

A place beyond the earthly sky
But deep within the soul
A pool is made of tears we cry
And written on the scroll

And as we grow the inner self
Will blossom from inside
The dross and gold together melt
Amid the rising tide

 And flooded now we reach the peak
And float upon the swell
The bitter blending with the sweet
Til heaven rings the bell

And prayer will lift and soothe the soul
Of all who speak and hear
And feel the pulse within the whole
Of all who gather near

And time will heal or so they say
And all time is right now
And Love will gather all who stray
And make all heads to bow

A Prayer

My spirit rose up with the sun
And bid the day hello
Lord, help me live with all I've done
And with all things here below

Give me strength to carry on
The good work you've assigned
But also let me have some fun
And let my love to shine

Pick me up when I am low
And hold me when I'm high
Teach my feet which way to go
And teach my heart to fly

Wrap me in your loving arms
But teach me how to soar
Protect me from all worldly harm
And guide me back to shore

Whisper in my ear to hear
The words you have for me
And make my vision very clear
That your face I may see

I Am

I am the scent upon the breeze
I am the sparkle in your eye
The tickle that has made you sneeze
The heart that never says goodbye

The thought that always makes you smile
The feeling that has made you sigh
The force that goes the extra mile
The colors that can paint the sky

I am the joy that causes tears
I am the pounding of the sea
I am the patience of the years
I am the buzzing of the bee

I am the roar of mighty cat
I am the moisture in the rain
I am the radar of the bat
I bring the children home again

The Chasm

The chasm of the great divide
Holds many souls so deep and wide
They're neither there and neither here
But lost and wander over there

Our prayer can lift them to the side
And God can feel the tears they cried
So pray for their immortal soul
For they are, too, part of the whole

And we are here, and we are one
We all must share what has been done
Lift each other, give a hand
Though shaky feet on shifting sand

And angels lend their buoyancy
When called upon by you and me
God didn't leave us helpless here
Upon this bright and shining sphere

Call on the mystic powers that be
Who live and breathe in harmony
Who hear the whispers of the heart
And feel the force love will impart

Shine

As time goes by and thoughts circle and land
Try to choose wisely and don't build on sand
Hold close to your heart the moments that cheer
Grateful and loving without doubt or fear

The law that attracts your manifestation
Is the law that can lift or conquer a nation
Choose clearly and wisely the words that you say
For the forces that be make them come back your way

Lift high your treasures to be of the soul
The thoughts that will flourish and nourish the whole
Let this be our prayer that we whisper each day
Thank God for the heavens that brighten our way

Surely a beacon a lamp to our feet
In the smile on the faces of those that we meet
A bright light within us that shines from the heart
A joy that is rising and shines in the dark

Seeds

As the thoughts that swirl and eddy
Whisper in my mind
Give way to focused thinking
I think I might just find

The path that has eluded me
One hidden by the weeds
One I myself had traveled once
And scattered all the seeds

So now I've come full circle back
And look for signs ahead
Have I ever really traveled here
Or dreamed this life instead

The Door

I feel the presence of a ghost
And wonder what he wants the most
And has he traveled very far
Is earth his home or distant star

May I help you I must ask
And have I known you in the past
Please let me know your business here
If you can please make that clear

The universe is ours, my friend
I see this journey has no end
And what we hear and what we see
Is just a dot in history

A tiny speck in the great whole
A tiny shadow of the soul
And with our blinders we can't see
Or feel the scope of what's to be

We're privy now to know the least
And when death comes life has not ceased
With a rush we're pushed once more
Through a once unopened door

Helping Hands

A student of the universe
Now clearly I can see
The spirits that escaped my sight
Now winking back at me

Surrounded always by their forms
They skip and fly and dance
Exquisitely they dance and sing
And bid me take a chance

A leap of faith on borrowed wings
They lead me by the hand
And joyfully they take the lead
Then gently we all land

A trip around the universe
Be brave and never fall
Their safety net is always there
For help we need but call

A warmth that holds my soul in hand
Now lifts me from the mire
I walk and run and fly sometimes
These days I never tire

Weave

In fairy tales and dreams we weave
The future we still can't conceive
And fate will bring what we believe
This does ring true don't be deceived

And what's around the corner now
Was once a thought within your brow
And time unfolds the things we dream
But as for now remains unseen

The deja vu you sometimes feel
Is like an ancient movie reel
The story written in your mind
A blueprint from a former time

Did you dream and did you see
But then forgot the memory
And is your mind the seat of soul
And will your heart still take control

And can this heart and mind be one
Or has our battle just begun
And when the nut falls from the tree
Can it foresee its mystery

The Shore

Joy and honor, sin and hate
All this we bring to heaven's gate
And all the seasons of the soul
Will fall and rise to meet the goal

And when the soul and Maker meet
The mission may be incomplete
To earth return the journey now
And heaven will assist somehow

The current deep beneath the wave
Returns to you all that you gave
Invisible, this mighty force
Will gently guide your every choice

And let His hand your rudder be
To steady you in stormy seas
Ask for love and nothing more
To guide you to the distant shore

Ask

I saw a waiting angel
Or was she just inside my head
I know I heard her call my name
And this is what she said

You've many here a trouble, child
Your past like a tattoo
Speaks to me of trials
And what you have been through

I read the lines upon your face
But mostly in your soul
You shield yourself from life's debris
That wash upon your shore

Your shyness does become you
When you bow your head in prayer
Though the forces of the cosmos
Hardly know you're there

And in your head you whisper
And you think that we can't hear
We're sharing every moment
And we're sharing every tear

So when you look around you
And you think you are alone
And you think we haven't found you
And you think you need your home

Divinity surrounds you
As on this earth you roam
Just ask and we will hear you
Amidst the ocean and the foam

The Wish

The shooting star passed by my wish
But blazed a path on heaven's slate
Your wants and needs are on the list
And now you only have to wait

And heaven knows just what you need
Your prayers have all been heard
And when you plant that tiny seed
It grows to mighty herb

Face of a Flower

Sunbeams brilliant flowing streams
Light up fluorescent flowers
They smile reflecting back the beams
And bask for many hours

Awakening with each new day
Soft dew upon the face
Their souls and all around them pray
Within their holy place

For surely God has made them all
As surely as they live
And loves them even when they fall
With nothing more to give

And they reflect the tender love
As it comes shining through
Their hearts all turned to God above
Reflecting back to you

New Start

My heart intense my soul aglow
I wonder if you see
The way you've made my heart to grow
When looking into me

I feel your glance you touch my soul
As only you can do
My broken heart is now made whole
Transformed because of you

I hear your voice it calms my mind
I deeply dream of you
Your arms' safe harbor now I find
Love coming into view

A longing tugging at my heart
I need our souls to meet
And we can make a brand new start
And life can be so sweet

Farewell

The shell of one who once had been
Displayed for all to see
The body empty, soul unseen
The tears I cry for me

They say a better place is he
This place up in the sky
But now the tears I cry for me
I'll always wonder why

And though a brighter day would come
If he'd just wait it out
Perhaps he heard a different drum
Perhaps there were no doubts

If this or that or other thing
Had been a different way
If I could heal a broken wing
If I'd known what to say

But all the "if's" are background now
To what had been his life
And all his earthly dreams are gone
But no more pain nor strife

But I shall miss the smile, the laugh
The twinkle of his eyes
But in this world we just see half
The soul dwells in the skies

Whispers of the Heart

Blessed happy sacred day
We meditate the dawn
With whispers of the heart we pray
For strength to carry on

This is the day the Lord hath made
Rejoice and be so glad
In sleeping dreams we've overstayed
Can waking be so bad

With outstretched arms we reach for Thee
And seek a guiding hand
We pray to Thee on bended knee
And pray the strength to stand

Our broken hearts we offer Thee
With spirits quite contrite
And pray Thee, mend me, make me see
The light in darkest night

Ever upward my desire
Is for my soul to fly
This my vision danced around
Upon my inward eye

For here within this dwelling place
This shell has housed my soul
And here I nightly meet the guides
And here my soul is whole

And freely dancing in the sky
My passion rose anew
I cross my heart and hope to die
When years are not too few

But for now I'll sing my song
And sing it with good cheer
And try to sing the tune I hear
Upon my inward ear

And countless prayers are reborn here
Within this central sphere
Within the sanctity of space
Where passion conquers fear

And though the path is long and steep
Although we're feeling faint
The Shepherd still will feed his sheep
All safe within His gates

The Return

A hazy cloud of light descends
And comes to claim my longtime friend
The gentle light caresses her
The soul within begins to stir

Gently upward spirit glides
Through the tunnel toward the sky
Surrounded by her spirit guides
Her soul remembers how to fly

Looking back, she sees her life
With all the love and all the strife
Thanking God she flies to Him
All's forgiven no more sin

What is sin but errors made
While in this land of sun and shade
But where she goes is only light
With no such thing as day or night

And many times she's made this trip
But always in a different ship
And what we need to know we learn
To ready us for our return

Across the Veil

In the sultry summer sun
My simmered soul did sweat
My mind was sinking, slowing down
To mode of deep regret

As memories were surfacing
While lying in this trance
My inward eye was turned to you
My partner in life's dance

And often in the quiet night
Your face appears in dreams
I wonder if you see me too
In the current of these streams

And if your soul is resting
Or tormented by the past
Or if you now have reconciled
Your final days at last

I wish that I could reach to you
And you could feel my touch
Will love always bind us up
This love that means so much

Perhaps you see these words I write
Perhaps you're always here
Sometimes I think I hear your thoughts
And feel that you are near

My heart embraces yours although
We reach across the veil
I hold you dear in inmost thoughts
Your breath still fills my sail

Colors

The stained glass window filters light
And each piece plays a part
The light within shines out at night
And brightens up the dark

And each of us our colors wear
And God gives of His light
The light is One for us to share
And keep each color bright

And many are the colors that
We individually wear
Vibrations are so varied yet
The white light holds us dear

In the sanctuary deep
The sunlight filters through
And brilliantly our colors meet
A spark from me to you

Wild Child

I thought about the two-edged sword
And both sides are so sharp
And of the concept of reward
Eternal fire or harp

And said methinks my Father will
Not torture any child
But patiently He guides until
His child is not so wild

Lovingly He shows the way
To make our light shine bright
Full grown we're happy to obey
That glowing inner Light

And freedom we will always have
The right to make a choice
And live our lives abundantly
And hear that inner voice

Earth Home

From earth to sky our words take wings
And breathe the breath of life to things
The word is breath and breath is life
And breath creates the thoughts we sigh

Mimosa blooms in silky pink
Appear the first of June
Their beauty makes me stop and think
My eyes caress the blooms

The kudzu vines now green and strong
Draped on the landscape here
Inspire my heart to sing a song
And fill my soul with cheer

The long and sunny afternoons
When thunderstorms pop up
Still fill my soul with grateful tunes
The music never stops

And when I breathe my final breath
In this my lifetime here
I know I'll miss the sparkling earth
The creatures all so dear

I know my heart will long to see
The clouds and clear blue sky
I'll long to climb a sturdy tree
And see the butterflies

Cicada's song in summer air
Hypnotic lullaby
Will draw me back to earth right here
We slept, but did not die

Again we find our way to earth
And love has drawn us here
The planet of our solar birth
The mission plan is clear

For love we must, and love will live
And always will survive
And love returns more than she gives
And God's within, alive

Rumbles

Upon the sun drenched deck I lie
Gazing up at cloudless sky
The breeze is blowing still but warm
No sign of close impending storm

The sounds of rustling trees above
The coo of distant morning dove
Reminds me Mother Nature hears
The sounds of days becoming years

And every sound that's ever heard
And every voice and every word
And every rumble of the earth
And every baby's cry at birth

The sound of waves that rush to shore
These sounds of nature will endure
The words that boosted strength to some
The words that made things come undone

The whisper of the heart will tell
The hollow chamber of the bell
Without this place the bell is naught
This structured space that man forgot

And deep inside your busy strife
Take time to stop and feel your life
And each moment that we breathe
The soul builds on what we believe

Be it joy or be it tears
Be it strength or be it fears
And in the diamond of your heart
Are many facets of your chart

And when we have each facet cleansed
The heart becomes a crystal lens
And finally we so clearly see
The spirit of how things should be

Our footsteps now are guided well
The compass in our soul can tell
The clear direction we must take
The choice is ours make no mistake

The inner voice of right and wrong
Is now a welcome guiding song
And gladly this the soul will hear
Hitch to this star and let Him steer

Listen

In quiet times the cream will rise
And float us to the top
We'll look on high at brighter skies
Where loving never stops

All things in place, all sorrows rest
The kingdom is right here
Where we reflect and manifest
Our thoughts within this sphere

Prepare the way to meet the day
When miracles will come
And hear what inner voices say
About "Thy will be done"

Align thyself with inner truth
Align thyself with Him
For you have known Him from your youth
And you have always been

Keep watch and daily pray for all
And speak to God on high
He listens daily to your call
And hears your every sigh

The saints and spirits listen in
And watch your every trial
They whisper guidance from within
And walk with you a while

So speak with them, they love your voice
When spoken from the heart
They'll help you with your every choice
And wisdom will impart

Transformation

Deep inside we all must tame
The rage the pain the fear
So call upon His Holy Name
Your vessel He must steer

This my heart I bare for you
And speaking of the truth
Rejected love had stripped me bare
While in my tender youth

With love betrayed I built a wall
To shield my heart from pain
Though unintentional this wall
Would seize my soul again

I let you chip just one brick out
And then another freed
But soon it caused the damn to break
I knew that I must flee

I saw a pattern, time to act
More pain, now came the fear
I never should have let you in
The pain was now too near

For in your hand you had my heart
Too trusting yet again
Was this just one more bad false start
Or are you my true friend

I got a glimpse when temper reared
Its awful ugly head
And got a sense that I should run
A feeling of pure dread

Your outer man, the one I love
Had soothed my wounded soul
But deep within I saw your rage
Another man came forth

He burst the image I had held
Of what true love should be
Reminded me of pain now past
And how I had to flee

And what can make a strong man act
So brutish with his rage
When on the surface it would seem
He had such loving ways

And how can woman reconcile
These two men she holds dear
The one that pleased and soothed the soul
The other planted fear

Real with You

You spoke to me with tender care
And let me know you're standing there
You whispered what I couldn't hear
But let me know you're with me, dear

The path I'm on is yours and mine
And sanctioned by a Love Divine
Please no more tears for when you cry
The clouds will gather in the sky

Rejoice for I have been released
My soul has found a higher peace
So mystified I found my fate
When heaven opened up her gate

My life did pass before my eyes
I felt your pain and heard your sighs
My heart awakened, then my brow
And everything was clear somehow

My soul rejoiced to be brought home
Where we are one, not dust and foam
And you are here within my soul
Another part of one great whole

I hear you breathe and see your smile
And I am with you all the while
Reflective quiet thoughts reveal
A greater depth where all is real

Brave Soldier of Life

A wounded soldier cried in pain
So far away from home
Cries rippled out and home again
I thought I heard him groan

Hearts may grieve the day of loss
For many nights to come
If we can die for one just cause
We suffer not alone

Beloved man hung on the cross
Of modern warfare pain
Can we recover what it costs
Or did he die in vain

Is this a lonely tear we cry
Or something we all share
And do we live the day we die
And will the soul be buried there

And finding comfort for the heart
When tortured deep the soul
And only God can then impart
The healing balm that make us whole

And that's where faith will enter in
And comfort souls who wait for Him
A knowing at the edge of mind
Will bubble up from time to time

Guided

The sun had bleached and purified
The darker thoughts I held inside
And chased them to a finer light
The light of God within the night

The Spirit lights the screen of mind
And brings to life the dreams that shine
In deep repose, the body still
The spirit walks and flies at will

We wander far to worlds unknown
But never take a step alone
Guided, loved, we are His child
The Father longs to see us smile

Blanched and tarnished we may be
And blinded to this mystery
The Father's plan will be revealed
But until then, remaining sealed

Time

As the second hand is sweeping
And tries to catch the first
And the broken heart is weeping
And we think we're through the worst

A calm and gentle presence
Lays His hand upon the heart
And we know that in our essence
We can never be apart

And as surely as the wind blows
And rivers go to sea
So deep within we must know
He gathers you and me

And all along the path now
The compass points to north
And though we may not know how
The spirit will shine forth

If ever we should hesitate
To know that God is near
So patiently we must wait
The heart must learn to hear

And deep within the visions
We view upon the bed
The Holy Spirit visits
By dreams we will be lead

Take a moment to remember
Each day when we arise
The spirit will surrender
Its gifts before our eyes

And in this time awaken
The joy from deep within
To know we're not forsaken
Or mired in our sin

The Good Lord He is risen
His hand we now must take
And Love imparts Her wisdom
Our sleeping soul must wake

The Flower

The flower opened with a smile
And looked into your eyes
Said sit with me a little while
And gaze at trees and skies

 Sit reflect and take a breath
And contemplate the day
For soon we pass on into death
And here we cannot stay

The page will turn the chapter ends
The story will go on
The Lord will bless each little flower
The words will turn to song

Solid Ground

An angel lifted high my head
And looked into my eyes
He brought me back though I was dead
And saw through my disguise

He lifted me and I could see
Him peer into my soul
He said you are what you must be
But God is in control

And just imagine little child
That God can really heal
Your body soul or mind gone wild
And deep within you feel

You know He can so pray He will
You stand on solid ground
But only God and Spirit heal
Just ask and health is found

World Without End

Beneath the sobering icy waters
My soul soon drifted to weigh what matters
My body frozen and too numb to feel
I left it behind to find what was real

I found myself floating up over the sea
And wondered aloud what's becoming of me
I saw myself clearly as never before
But seeking to plant my feet firmly on shore

There was shouting and chaos and crying and pain
And many souls with me still striving in vain
The ship now was sunken no trace of her hull
The voices grew silent the world now looked small

I found myself drifting aloft in deep space
The earth far below me, my path I can't trace
And further I flew as if pushed by a glove
Reflecting on earth and the heavens above

The journey's not over and this was quite clear
Though I don't know the time nor the date nor the year
And yet I remember this death from the past
And now we're together again on the mast

Clinging to life at the top of the ship
As it lunges and rolls and we know it will flip
And we're all going down to the dark sea below
'Til the Spirit's released by The Archer's bow

The Archer sees with clarity
Projects a path for you and me
And we will both be sent again
The world is truly without end

Always

I roamed in fields of daffodils
Within your deep blue eyes
And drinking in my spirit fills
And knows of no surprise

A clever and seductive trip
I let you board the mother ship
And we both laughing took the plunge
And skies were opened, bells were rung

And tenderly you lead me there
A path carved out by dreams
You tipped your hat and paid your fare
And conquered other streams

The gift you gave me, precious life
Now bloomed our own sweet child
The years have come and long gone since
The days of free and wild

The clock ticks down to closing days
We've ten or twenty more
Yet through the years and through the haze
We long for distant shores

Somehow the circle closing now
Will roll and spin and take a bow
Forever joined in love it's clear
Though far away, you're always near

And where we go the door will stop
Regret and guilt and pain
And only love can enter in
And pass this way again

Sleepy Morning

Misty gray and morning sky
Whispered hush and lullaby
Fragments of a nighttime dream
Imprinted on mind's inner screen

And like an old lost movie reel
They come to life and so reveal
The rivers where the spirits flown
And manifest with seeds we've sown

Every

Every hair upon your head
And every little bird
Every tear you ever shed
And every little word

Every whisper in the night
And every shadow cast
Every flicker of your light
And every wartime blast

Every heartache, every tear
All your happy smiles
All the sound upon your ear
And every little trial

Every night and every day
Marked along the path
Illumined by a brand new way
So bring your rod and staff

And clearly He will guide you
And clearly you are dear
He'll wrap you in His mantle
There's nothing left to fear

I'll See You

A tender trace of salty tears
Has dampened all my heart
I've longed to hold your breast to mine
These years we've been apart

Your smile, your voice, your tender words
Still echo in my mind
I visit you in memory
You always will be mine

So often whispered prayers of you
Rise upward to the sky
I miss you more each passing year
I'll see you when I die

Longing

An ancient song of happy love
Still smolders in my heart
I wonder how the years have flown
Since we have been apart

It's all too quiet in the house
Where we were next of kin
I miss your love, your warm embrace
Your understanding grin

It seems a lifetime, long ago
Although it's just been years
My heart would watch yours in the dark
So full with happy tears

My longing grows much deeper now
I reach for you in dreams
The silence of the lonely nights
Absorbs my silent screams

Time

Your fingers interweave with mine
Your heart in harmony keeps time
Time, an abstract situation
Replies at once in indignation

For all the time you have is now
The time to reap, the time to plow
The present moment captures you
The past is only for review

The future you expect won't come
The song within you will be sung
The drama played out to the end
With luck, you'll share it with a friend

Search your soul and act with love
Or nothing keeps our heads above
The waves that toss us on the sea
For only love brings buoyancy

A Past Life

I knew you in the days gone by
I saw your tears and heard you cry
Barefoot on the cobblestone
You stumbled desperately alone

Your warm blood poured from gaping wounds
Your sobs the sound of hopeless tunes
So suddenly your spirit fled
And hovered over fleshly dead

How thankful, grateful, thrilled I was
To be released by God above
A life of suffering I had seen
A disillusioned girl I'd been

Brutally stabbed and thrown in the street
But death came to me as a welcome release
That life had been sad and I longed to go home
And sit by the side of the heavenly throne

That death was so swift and I was so young
That life had been hard, I was tired to the bone
I never did hit that cobblestone street
My spirit escaped while still on my feet

Adrift

If you were buried deep in hell
And wishing for a wishing well
There would always some hope be
Remember wishing is for free

Dreams become a thing of choice
And God can hear the smallest voice
And if the heart emits a sigh
It registers with God on high

If I had a way to grieve
The love from which I take my leave
My wounded heart could heal the scar
That runs so deep and oh, so far

Miracle of wondrous earth
That reclaims all with deadly mirth
We choose to rally one last flight
One more long and lonely night

One more chance to ease the pain
Calling on our Father's name
When through the grains of life I sift
I find so much has gone adrift

Two steps forward, three steps back
I search for love, 'tis love I lack
I fell soul deep in foreign land
Where hearts were cold and love was bland

I longed for home, the brilliant light
My tears wrung out in endless night
I search the sky for signs of dawn
Full circle swings our warming sun

Traces

Traces of a day gone by
Arose and touched that inner eye
I witnessed in a morning dream
And felt the pull of long lost things

I reached to hold an ancient love
Protect him from I knew not what
I saw that he's a baby now
The size of me but yet somehow

He's tall and dark with thick-maned brow
I groomed him, loved him long ago
And now he is a tiny foal
This love a handsome horse I know

I held him in my dream today
And offered him alfalfa hay
Caressed his neck and stroked his mane
And wished him here with me again

Circles

Your angel heart and silent grin
Bid my soul to come on in
We met and chatted for a while
But all along I knew that smile

Flashes from so long ago
Flickered bright and lit my soul
Yes, we had met somewhere before
A distant time and distant shore

And much like water magnetized
We flow together hypnotized
For I have loved you in the past
And memories will always last

Oh mighty Master, this we know
No matter where, how far we go
We're caught like fish within the net
A bit unsure, not knowing yet

The plan has saved us from ourselves
Hypnotized by magic spells
Believing all that we can see
Not knowing that we could break free

For so much more there is to life
Than sounds we hear and things in sight
So limited our five sense world
With so much more to yet unfold

All a swirl of harmony
And spinning synchronicity
Circles that will have no end
We'll ride the current with a friend

Falling in with ancient flow
Cycles where we reap and sow
Impulse leads us by a hair
Our every thought has lead us there

Like tiny threads we interweave
We're in and out but never leave
For all the dead are standing there
Between the walls of light and air

Like tiny angels we can't see
Become the friends of you and me
And whisper sometimes on the wind
Insightful thoughts that they can send

And often in the quiet night
Imagery of dreams so bright
And buoyancy will take us where
The soul can rest without a care

The Walk-In

Alas, I saw your other face
Relaxed, but in a trance
A character of your embrace
Who, with your soul, will dance

Departed from your mother's son
An entity stands near
And takes your place, sometimes for fun
And robs you of your cheer

Get thee behind me Satan's friend
From you I stand apart
I do not wish to see the end
Of your split tortured heart

The Dirt You Gave Me

As I was walking through the door
My heart leaped in relief
I won't see you anymore
I leave behind this grief

No more heartbreak, no more tears
Will follow me around
No more living in such fear
I'm breaking brand new ground

The dirt you gave me I won't keep
I'm shaking off the dust
My battered heart has gone to sleep
Long gone is any trust

My address changed, I'll venture far
So far away from you
Looking to my guiding star
Beginning life anew

I didn't kill you though I could
For all you did to me
It wouldn't do me any good
I wouldn't now be free

I didn't slash or burn your stuff
Just karma stopping me
This torn up heart has had enough
Just needed to be free

And now each night I go to sleep
Just calm and feeling safe
My soul and sanity I keep
So well since my escape

With years gone by, I heard you died
The scary monster dead
And wonder if the demons slide
Into another's head

You let them in with too much drink
And too much coke and smack
They stole your thoughts, the way you think
You never got it back

And if we ever meet again
Beyond the afterlife
I'll pray your demons have an end
And have been exorcized

They took a man that once was good
And tore him down to naught
And if you could, I know you would
A better battle fought

I Love You More

My heart beat fast like a runaway train
When I heard you close the door
Is there a time when I'll see you again
Or will I not see you anymore

Duty calls or so they say
When they send you off to war
Oh my lord, is there no other way
But to fight on a foreign shore

I love my country, but I love you more
Sometimes all alone I cry
Will you come back, I can never be sure
Only sure I may surely die

A Visit

A wisp of air that kissed my face
Made me long for your embrace
I felt you here so near yet far
You vanished like a shooting star

Dedicated to my loving daughter and best friend, Tuesday,
whose bright and charming spirit has been
the greatest blessing of my life.

Jewels of the Night

Aching eyes too long asleep
Reject the light of dawn
We look within for one last peek
At dreams before they're gone

Awaken now, let go the jewels
Belonging to the night
Your dreams are only subtle tools
To guide you toward the light

Echoes

In darkness sat I by myself
Peering through the air
And lo, my sense did gather in
A presence in my lair

My sight did strain to grasp the thing
I fancied I did see
A burst of echoes from my thought
Came bouncing back at me

The Tune

Vast company surrounding me
Advise me of the truth
And sing to me the melody
That carried me through youth

I've heard the tune, I know the words
Of songs that can't be sung
Cathedrals hum inside my mind
Where holy bells have always rung

The Voice

Father, I would ask of Thee
That Thou wouldst give me heart
Enough to love each loving soul
Of which I am a part

Grant for me my silent prayer
That your voice will be heard
Upon the earth and everywhere
Each sweet and loving word

The Chorus

A voice, a whisper, sang to me
A sound like waves upon the sea
I hear it in the quiet times
The purring of a cosmic rhyme

An insect chorus late at night
Humming, soothing lullaby
In the silent world within
The ever-present chorus sings

Time Unfolds

Like an inner cosmic light
My dreams light up my darkest night
And like a beacon from within
Warns me of impending sin

They guide me down the winding trail
And let me glimpse behind the veil
We learn the secrets of beyond
First the words and then the song

The sweeping hand of time doth tell
The secrets of the wishing well
And tho' her depths be silent, deep
Time unfolds the dreams we keep

And wondrous mysteries we've half known
Reveal themselves, become full blown
And all our love will one day be
The master force that turns the key

Buoyant Hope

Now I lay me down to sleep
I pray the Lord one tiny peek
A spark of love to light my scope
And bring me fresh and buoyant hope

Clean Snow upon the Dirt

A deeply gnawing pain I felt
A torture to my soul
One moment more my heart will melt
I still can feel the sword

Burst wide my core
And scatter far the memory of the hurt
Erase, that there will be no scar
Clean snow upon the dirt

Upon the brightness of the snow
The sun will spread his beams
One moment more and we will know
The meaning of our dreams

And in the melting of the cold
The soul will be quite clear
And tho' the heart be very old
It knows not any fear

And thus in strength the journey now
Will lead us to our home
And happiness for knowledge gained
From all the time we roamed

I Would Request of Thee

Dear Father, show me how to love
Without a single fear
Let me pour my all upon
All those within my sphere

Rejection, though, I've often met
It's wounded deep my soul
Yet the scars are almost gone
Your love hath made me whole

Though meanings might seem so obscure
Reflection makes things clear
A little time and we are sure
Just why we shed each tear

Patience leads her children home
Don't question on the way
But lovingly accept the good
And Love's voice do obey

Father, lift us high above
What we think our needs to be
Lift us high and let us know
That all we need is Thee

Yesterday Tomorrow Today

What matters now the frosted grass
The open trenches, deadly blast
The battle's o'er, the smoke's cleared 'way
The gleaming sun's baptized the day

What matters now the blood and pain
The suffering was not all in vain
We need not relive yesterday
Altho' 'twas just a breath away

For yesterday was just a dream
Tomorrow holds her breath unseen
Today's the place where we must be
Unchain the past and be set free

Away Untimely Death

Death, sweet death, please wait for me
Until the time my soul flies free
Wean me then from Mother Earth
The planet of my solar birth

But greet me not with downcast face
And sorrow, let there be no trace
But happily, I'll leave this shell
Where spirit can no longer dwell

So far away, so far from here
Above the highest stratosphere
Where nothing like our gravity
Can lure me down again from Thee

Away, untimely death, don't call
'Til I can rise above it all
And bid me not 'til I have done
The things for which my soul hath come

The Shining Light

Tho' black clouds loom so dark and large
They block the sun and hide the stars
They cannot stop the shining light
The sun by day nor moon by night

The light will shine forever clear
Above the earth's small atmosphere
Illusive darkness cannot stay
But must give way to light of day

So hold on tight, await the dawn
The skies will clear and spring will come

All Time To Grow

Now I know 'tis wise indeed
Not to long for every need
But rather, patience, set aglow
Will answer, in the end, we'll know

And all our needs, they will be met
Through wasted moments we will fret
But wiser now, we soon will be
Though patience is the only key

Serenity, that deep down peace
Soothes the heart and stills the beast
Tranquility, that quiet mood
Frees the soul that used to brood

For why should we who used to fret
Be anxious over any debt
Or worry over any woe
When we've all time, all space to grow

A Bit of Leaven

Caught in nature's love embrace
I thought I saw my Maker's face
A thousand facets of Him shone
Don't ever think you are alone

So many times, so many ways
We look around and meet His gaze
The spirits of the life we see
Vibrate in perfect harmony

A song of triumph, joy complete
Amazing grace that is so sweet
And with a bit of leaven rise
On wings of love above the skies

Rise Above

As the evening sun does sink
Amid her final rays
And night's shadow nestles near
We turn within and learn to pray

For out of darkness comes the need
Of searching for the light
And when our prayers reach higher tones
We rise above the veil of night

And speedily we see the day
Which always has been there
Above the clouds, above the air
And penetrating everywhere

Summer

Birdsong on a summer's morn
Makes me glad that I was born
Cicada's song up in the trees
Really puts my soul at ease

Lightning bolts that light the sky
Teach me of a God on high
The sound of thunder rumbling long
Adds the bass to summer song

Mimosa trees now in full bloom
Warm nights to witness stars and moon
Balmy breezes, sticky air
Summer flowers everywhere

And lightning bugs, my heart's delight
Special treasure of the night
Warm sun soaked up by the skin
Warms the heart so deep within

The graceful flitting butterfly
Adds her colors to the sky
Water beckons us to swim
To row our boats and live life's dream

Berries ripened in the sun
Our fellow creatures raising young
The chorus of the croaking frogs
Add to summer's dialogue

The flowers welcome bees right in
They know their joy and not their sting
Hazy light of summer's dawn
Dispels the mist and heat grows strong

The sun beams drench in summer gold
The colors now shine bright and bold
In evening's quiet we may sigh
And rest in nature's lullaby

June bugs crash on window glass
And, oh, the smell of fresh mown grass
All the trees wear summer green
While autumn holds her breath unseen

Ice cream, snow cones, lemonade
Looking for a patch of shade
From the garden, melons, squash
These are things I love so much

Wings of Faith

On wings of faith the soul can fly
Soaring buoyantly so high
Truly faith remains supreme
The master builder of a dream

High above the stratosphere
I gazed upon deep space
The stars and planets bright and clear
I thought I saw my Maker's face

I met two strangers in my path
I told them to have faith
And then when they began to laugh
Before their eyes I flew away

I called to them, "What think you now?"
"Have you ever flown so high?"
Listen, take my words to heart
And soon one day you'll fly

God's Tapestry

Reflected in the sphere of dew
I saw the world made all brand new
So innocent and clear it was
So bright and perfect, free from flaws

And in an instant, vaporize
Vanished upward to the skies
For just a moment we were here
And in the next we disappeared

Vanquished to another plane
Forgetting all our earthly pain
And like children grown at last
We reap the fruit of all things past

For all things now and all things seen
Are part of what has always been
And in our dreams we hold the key
Of what is now and what's to be

So let us now embrace the light
Before it's taken from our sight
And quickly we may fly away
And none of us will know the day

But this we know, the time will come
When earth and sea and sky are one
The fabric of the universe
Has every thread upon its course

And all are joined in harmony
Weaving God's own tapestry
Together sing and take a chance
Together bonded in Love's dance

Cosmic Dust

Oh, Father of the earth and sky
I seek and wonder, years go by
I doubt too often cry too long
But always I return with song

But try me, break me, if You must
Scatter me like cosmic dust
For in the wind, Your love will blow
And give the dust a sacred glow

The Harvest

As summer dawns and spring abates
The driving wind within the gates
Doth gain the entrance to our time
And man doth learn of love divine

Oh, sudden glory, welcome home
You've come to claim your royal throne
And cast me down beside your feet
And reap my golden grain of wheat

Oh, ripened grape upon the vine
'Tis time to reap you for the wine
The sunshine blossomed in your skin
And now shines outward from within

And slowly, tho' you know not why
The tears of clouds within you cry
Your heart is pierced and love doth flow
And now you drink the wine of Soul

The Empty Shell

Like seashells bleached out in the sun
The life within has been and gone
No longer bound to spiral shell
An empty house the shell is now

The silver cord is loosed on high
The spirit's free to fly the sky
So do not mourn for empty shells
When heaven calls and rings her bells

But thankful that a soul was freed
Who lives on now beyond the sea

Solitude

Tho' solitude is sad for some
I relish time to be alone
A chance to touch the inner soul
Reflect and heal and be made whole

The Center

Amid the raging storm of mine
There lies a center deep inside
Where strife lives not and truth is calm
And all our paths become as one

And all that's real becomes so clear
We've heard it said love casts out fear
How true it is so take to heart
The love we seek is near, not far

He Is Nigh

Happy sprouts out wings to fly
And beckons you, don't pass it by
Love frees you in a bright blue sky
And blesses you to know God's nigh

He's nearer than your own heartbeat
He walks with you upon your feet
He breathes with you each living breath
He dwells in you and knows no death

He knows no panic or disease
He's power over all of these
He loves you, you're His own offspring
He loves you more than anything

Manifestations

A dream popped up inside my head
I'm not sure where it's from
It speaks to me of strange new things
My own mouth is so dumb

Ideas flow within my soul
And manifest in time
Grown from thought, a little seed
Maturing like fine wine

To waste the mind with petty thoughts
Is really such a shame
For what we think, we do produce
With only thoughts to blame

Touch the Stars

O'er the mountain so afar
Lingered there a brilliant star
My mouth agape, I watched it climb
It split the earth, devoured time

A twinkling of the eye they say
Can share a secret stored away
And in a moment's glance, it beams
And joins in life two living streams

And if a glance ignites a spark
And light is better than the dark
Can we not climb to reach the heights
And touch the stars that dot the nights

Oh, fancy, pretty, happy dreams
The mighty river's made of streams
A shining sea of pregnant swells
Will wash the shores where love does dwell

New Age Sun

The midday sun was rising
And burned the mist away
This midday sun was brighter
Than any other day

The shadows all were shorter
Than ever they had been
The light reached every crevice
Without and deep within

The creatures of the darkness
Had nowhere dark to run
They fled before each racing beam
Of this new brightened sun

The fears and all ill feelings
Dissolved before such love
'Twas nowhere they could linger
The age had pushed them on

And banished was all evil
'Twas love in everyone
And every soul within them knew
That they had found their sun

The Serpent

Let the dreaming serpent sleep
All comatose with sleep so deep
And wake him not with morning bell
For all his dreams are dreams of hell

Life is dreaming crystallized
As thought forms dance before our eyes
Made manifest on walls of time
They fall in place like words of rhyme

The wily serpent raised his head
But only for his skin to shed
And tho' he didn't try to strike
Man thought he did and raised the spike

The serpent died upon his bed
The spike was thrust right through his head
His evil reputation lives
And grants that we no mercy give

The Rending of the Veil

How do we deal with the blow of death
That preys on us with icy breath
The soul springs free with great expansion
And leaves behind its earthly mansion
The veil is lifted for the deceased
And we await, not yet released

And yea, my soul could fly with ease
And soar upon the smallest breeze
But here I must remain at last
And set about my earthly task

Don't ask who sees the way you see it
Ask what's good and then just be it
Pursue your loves whate'er they be
And your heart will set you free

Once 'twas known as blasphemy
To know how near is God to thee
A future waits beside your star
Reveals itself and who you are

Dreams Without Number

Quiet moments of reflection inside
Time to acknowledge the love that we hide
Tranquil waves caress our souls
Time to evaluate all of our goals

Sweetest sleep of dream state slumber
Crossing our minds are dreams without number
Lovely blessed refreshing sleep
Instills serenity very deep

Daily circumstance comes to light
During the darkness of the night
Flashes of future scenes seem to ascend
Things we've expressed that we must amend

A Cloud

If I were a cloud and my essence was dew
I'd love the advantage of heavenly view
I'd gently squeeze drops from my delicate frame
And I'd invite lightning to light up the game
I'd welcome the thunder that follows the flash
I'd relish the roar, the magnificent blast

The Glass Darkly

I humbly beseech Thee oh, Lord up above
To shine down Thy beauty, Thy truth, and Thy love
I ask for Thy guidance and in a loud voice
To ring in my ears and assist in my choice
For through the glass darkly, I dimly perceive
We bring to our lives what we firmly believe

Loving Guidance

Sweet enduring Father of the grass
and of the tree
I get a flowing feeling to know you
care for me
Dear Mother of the stars and of our
own sweet land
I know that You're all Love when you
take me by the hand
'Tis such a deep communion to listen
to your thoughts
To know of all the great things Your
loving hand has wrought
Sweep us with your majesty beyond your
highest slopes
Guide us ever upward far past our
dreamy hopes

Metamorphosis

The caterpillar saw no death
He changed from deep inside
He waited on God's loving hand
Yes, God his only guide

Let us shed our mortal skin
And be reborn from deep within
Emerging like the butterfly
With pure new wings to soar on high

Skeptics there are many
And some would see me fail
But I've learned to ride the wind
And use it for my sail

Life is but an awesome storm
That's quiet at the center
Find this place and you will know
The Kingdom you have entered

An Empty Vessel

When mind, body, and soul agree
'Tis only then that we soar free
Divine power expands from within
Dispersing, correcting every sin

When Father, Son, and Ghost are one
Light fills the soul like the midday sun
Serenity comes like a newfound friend
And opens the gates of heaven within

Oh, Lord of lords, I ask of Thee
My soul prostrate on bended knee
This longing in my heart doth rise
Amid my sobs and heaving sighs

An empty vessel I am now
My heart contrite, a broken bough
Fill me with Thy Holy Ghost
And help me keep my watchful post

How long I've known my path to keep
Too often straying like a sheep
Receive me now, I'm coming home
For I have wandered far too long

Farewell Flight

I'll be okay without you now
I've learned to live and love somehow
A new life I have come to know
And toward the light we all must grow

Upward, ever upward bound
We leave behind the cold hard ground
With wings outstretched reach for the sky
Catch the wind and learn to fly

A dozen arrows pierced my heart
And bid my soul to flee
Another thousand I'll depart
And take my heart with me

For none may strike that lethal blow
Before my time is ripe
And none may stop the shining sun
From giving of her light

I thought of all who have gone on
Beyond the veil and past the sun
A singing memory of their love
A quiet longing for The Dove

The Dove of Peace who comes on wings
And sings of all the love He brings
So welcome Him, His flight's been long
Cherish Him and drink His song

My Sword

I set my foot upon the shore
So long I was at sea
And there before me was a door
Another choice for me

Assisted by my Lord's own angels
I stepped into this world
A life of many trials and tangles
Faith & love my only sword

But always with me to the end
The angel's love and more
My faithful Jesus, loving friend
The one whom I adore

Through every trial, every trouble
I've been safe within His hand
His angels lift me when I stumble
And steady me on shifting sand

The Friendly Stranger

It came to me from deep despair
I met a friendly stranger there
He urged me come, and share his peace
And put behind me all my grief

A gentle hand persuaded me
And bid me come, commune with Thee
Be not afraid, I heard him say
For love is with you all the way

We care not what your sins may be
For Love, the King, has made you free
No longer servant to your sin
Serve only God and enter in

In silence, you must keep your tongue
And let your song within be sung
And glorify the Love Divine
And let that Love just shine and shine

The Awakening

A restless mind can wander far, aloft on
muddy dreams
But clarity will visit only peace of mind
it seems
A brilliant light my mind did see, a color
blazing radiantly
A tone so fierce, a depth so deep
awoke my soul, so long asleep
Silent, gliding, shifting time, you bring
about the birth
Of all the thoughts we hold inside on God's
small, sparkling earth
And tho' our minds are far from wise, we've
conjured up this spell
And made our dreams to crystallize within
the space we dwell
A welling rose up from my soul and
wretched out all my sin
Replacing it with love made whole
awakened God who slept within
Awareness made so sharply keen, now
longs for brilliant light
And wonders how we've ever lived amid
the darkened night

Doubting Thomas

Arise and get up from the dirt
Comb your hair and change your shirt
Prepare thyself to meet the King
To be His love and wear His ring

Patiently you've sought His face
And longed to know His love and grace
Quickly rise, He's at the door
And seeks to lift thee from the floor

Oh, doubting heart, He knows thee well
Yet thee, like Thomas, He will tell
Touch me, feel me, thou shalt see
The Love that sets the captives free

Out On A Limb

Oh, angel of death, connect us to Him
For often we find ourselves out on a limb
Teach us to hear the words that He speaks
Help us to know He'll give what we seek

Blessed relief to know that He hears
A calm water quenches all of our fears
As light grows dim and dark comes upon us
We reach to the light that shines ever on us

Always knowing our every need
Assisting us 'til at last we are freed
With the angel of death the body's forsaken
This life we have dreamed but finally awaken

Oh, beautiful Maker, we know You at last
Your form is exquisite, Your love more than vast
The gift You have given, we've known not 'til now
We've been the fine rain of a heavenly cloud

Dust to Dust

Box me not in metal case
I want but just a sheet
No fancy dress nor ornaments
Nor shoes upon my feet

Tie no tag upon my toes
And leave my shell intact
Bury me with my own blood
Not fluid from a chemist's rack

All I need is earth's cool ground
Caressing all my limbs
A place to let my blood to seep
Dispersing all my sins

Rejoined to dust in nuptials
Rejoined likewise to God
'Tis with great pleasure I return
This temple to the sod

Life's been good but death's so sweet
With better things to come
I only hope that when I leave
There's nothing left undone

Little Moments

Magical moments refreshing as dew
Clothes each new scene with mystical hues
Enchanting the forest and all that's in view
Exposing a side of things we never knew

Looking at life with new and clear eyes
It's such a sweet wonderful happy surprise
Engulfed in a bondage of clever disguise
We're free at last when we see through the lies

Older than ancient the sages have told
A story so long that never unfolds
A small little truth each day can be seen
Another sweet gem to add to your dream

Never the end will come into view
Each little moment refreshes anew

By Our Own Hand

I have no grudge against you
It isn't mine to bear
You've never sinned against me
You've never harmed a hair

We only sin against ourselves
'Tis hard to understand
And if we get a taste of hell
'Tis by our own dear hand

If heaven opens up for us
And very well it may
'Tis just the offspring of our love
For love's the only way

Legion of Angels

Floating on a wisp of air
I thought I saw some angels there
Sweet and easy in their flight
Knowing not of day or night

New perception gaining ground
Listening to a brand new sound
Humbly lay I by Thy feet
Not ever knowing love so sweet

Nestled in Thy loving breast
Finally finding sweetest rest
Rising in the summer sky
Bands of angels always nigh

Binding Love

Help me, help me was the cry
I couldn't turn my ear away
I'll come to thee if I must fly
I couldn't tell thee nay

For what is life but sharing love
And helping with the task
Of helping others like ourselves
Before they need to ask

For laws of love do bind themselves
Upon our very souls
And bless us with those happy spells
As life within unfolds

Immortal

Immortal though we all may be
Our lives come to an end
But then the spirit flies so free
The road we're on must bend

With each new turn our soul must make
We'll surely need a friend
And try to give more than we take
This journey has no end

Before our birth, the soul exists
In future as in past
And in the present moment's kiss
Beyond the door called death we last

Forever in the scheme of things
Our love it shall endure
In family, spouse, pets, and friends
Immortal I am sure

Terminal Velocity

When I skydive
I arrive
At a place where my speed carries me

When I free fall
To nowhere at all
And my spirit is suddenly free

When I look down
To the ground
With the sound of air rushing past my ear

I know that I'll be
Forever free
And conquering every fear

Thoughts Take Wings

I glimpsed inside the secret chamber
Gently knocking at the door
I asked that my name be remembered
For loving God and nothing more

The secret brotherhood inside
Made a note of tears I cried
They said my pleas were often heard
And that God heard every word

They said, now go, and gather strength
And guard the sacred thoughts you think
For thoughts that orbit crystallize
And manifest before our eyes

So fill your heart with loving things
And truly do these thoughts take wings
And come full circle back at last
To flower on your earthly path

Times Remembered

I crossed the sea where I believed
My body cold and drowned
And trod the path where I had thought
Me buried in the ground

I walked on cobblestones where once
My blood was spilled one night
And I remembered many things
The spirit taking flight

And once I was a soldier
Who died on foreign land
Quite surprised that death had come
And gained the upper hand

So many times on Mother Earth
My soul returned like spring
After bitter winter's cold
Had done her deadly thing

For every season under God
The cycle marches on
As surely as the darkened night
Is followed by the dawn

Magnetic Force

Raindrops fall like liquid bombs
And devastate the dusty calms
And from the view of one so small
A dewdrop is a giant ball

And larger spheres that orbit space
Move perfectly within their place
And all are balanced, moving free
With graceful speed and certainty

Invisible magnetic force
You have each orb upon its course
You bring the mist that brings the rain
You call the soul back home again

You teach the birds to fly the breeze
And move the mighty tides with ease
You are, to me, the purest wings
That lift me over earthly things

Invisible Wind

Miracles in daily life
Go unnoticed 'mongst the strife
Our ears turn dull and eyes don't see
The sparkle and the majesty

The gentle swaying of the breeze
Brings shimmer to the tiny leaves
The tree then speaks a sighing sound
It's whisper echoes from the ground

And if we listen we will hear
A magic voice that casts out fear
A song that has no outer sound
But lifts us right up off the ground

So do not close your eyes to these
Your eyes cannot perceive the breeze
But they can see what wind can do
The ears can hear the wind song too

Little moments of the day
When miracles have paved the way
Unfold and blossom in their time
And sing to us of love divine

Turn Within

Amid the clamor of the day
We take the time to rest and pray
Recharge our spirit and reflect
Put aside our every debt

Let it go, it matters not
For look at all His hand has wrought
The spacious sky, the earthly nest
The space beyond, we have the best

Think not on things that we have not
But of all the good we've got
The sparkling sea and precious love
Refreshing breezes, birds above

Fragrant flower, grazing beast
Sparkling stars, and last, not least
The angels of the earth and air
Who live among us everywhere

The angels of the sea and sun
Who stay with us til day is done
Who cradle us when we're asleep
Who guide us through the valley deep

So whisper this your daily prayer
And know that God is everywhere
Within your heart, within your soul
He holds the power to make you whole

So listen deeply, hear His song
Although the road is rough and long
He'll bear you up lest you should fall
And soon you'll rise above it all

Your heart will sing and sorrow heal
Your tears will water fertile fields
The seeds of doubt will disappear
The seeds of love will conquer fear

And when the light of love shines bright
It brightens up the darkest night
Celestial music, cosmic hum
Soothes the soul, outshines the sun

Love Regained

Deep inside my memory
I recognized your face
Although it was another time
And in another place

I treasured you as I do now
And lovers we were then
That longing lived inside my heart
And sang a lover's hymn

My gratitude to find you now
Gives daily praise to God
My soul is full right to the brim
And overflows with love

Where Are You?

Slipping through the silent wave
An iridescent smile you gave
The ocean foam caressed your face
I rushed to feel your warm embrace

Alas! It was but just a dream
A vision my mind's eye had seen
This hollow place within my heart
Seeks to know its counterpart

When I remember what I know
And feel the love from long ago
My memory will return to thee
And bless the time when we were free

My homeland calls, the time draws near
I may not stay another year
I'm lonely for the Master's touch
And all the love that means so much

Blueprint

In the quietness of solitude
While in an introspective mood
I charm myself with fantasy
And weave the dreams of what's to be

Entranced was I, but still asleep
I knew this dream was one I'd keep
A nagging thought, a memory
Had cloaked itself in mystery

Revealing life between the lines
Foretelling all our future times
Unveiling all the secret things
Forecasting all the winds of change

Trust the dreams for they will guide
And keep us buoyant in the tide
Instructing us at every turn
And sealing all we ever learn

Imprinted deep within the soul
The blueprint that can make us whole
The secret of the master plan
One day will be revealed to man

Inward Glance

A gallant hope, a faded dream
A memory vague of things unseen
Instructions from the Maker's sleep
Reveal the thoughts that thunder deep

Though deep within they are, yet far
A brilliant treasure like a star
And when this journey nears an end
That star will be a long lost friend

And face to face with it, at last
A dazzling glimpse into the past
The veil concealing things unknown
Will open wide to bid you home

Inward glance, do I know me
My highs and lows a tidal sea
The waves of time wear down my shore
Yet I will be forevermore

Though my form may always change
The "me" inside remains the same
I've always been, I'll always be
A spirit soaring high and free

Tree Spirit

I spent an hour in a tree
With all her leaves embracing me
I did this daily through my youth
And found it was a path to truth

The breeze would sway the limbs and me
And for this hour my mind was free
I'd wander far from earth in time
And glimpse a meaning so sublime

A total rest I had up there
Just me, the tree, and sky, and air
I long to climb a tree again
And perch upon a sturdy limb

And from up there this birds' eye view
Refreshes and makes all things new
The tree has spirit she'll impart
And whispers straight into your heart

But, ah, to be a youth again
To have a tree as my best friend
To take the time to dream a dream
And contemplate the things unseen

You know we must return at last
Arrive full circle from the past
We shape the future starting now
We hold the past within our brow

So stop and rest in mighty trees
And let your thoughts drift on the breeze
Expanding upward through the sky
A tear of rapture floods my eye

Knowledge Remembered

'Twas just a dim dark memory
My mind had pushed aside
A long forgotten melody
That song from deep inside

The tune returned and then the words
Now played upon my ear
And on the inward eye came forth
The vision of a seer

Test your wings and try to fly
Test your blues to match the sky
Cry for love and finding none
Warm the moon and cool the sun

The summer moon lit up the sky
A gentle wind blew through
In all the years of asking why
So suddenly I knew

Peace Be Still

A little whisper in my ear
Like music on the sea
In quiet times it's louder still
Spinning wheels in harmony

I close my eyes and visions dance
Upon this inner screen
A great cathedral is the mind
Where angels always sing

But to hear them we must learn
To quiet down our thoughts
Yes, listen hard and peace be still
And know that I am God

The Promise

Nightly on the screen of mind
Instructions come to me
And all the ways that I've been blind
Are lighted up and now I see

Daily as l rise to greet
The coming of the day
I have this promise I can keep
That love will light the way

And when my path becomes too steep
I know that help will come
Whenever I am feeling weak
I know He'll make me strong

So keep the faith and know the path
Takes turns we don't foresee
And help will come if we will ask
And guide us home to Thee

The End?

The blazing sun that caught my eye
Knew my secrets, heard my sighs
Nothing was not known to Him
All my triumph, all my sin

All my joys and all my tears
All my dreams throughout the years
I couldn't hide a single thing
But suddenly was gone all pain

My lungs had heaved a final breath
My now still heart awaited death
But there I was, above it all
My spirit soared, I was in awe

So death was but to shed a skin
Emerge refreshed from deep within
And like the lovely butterfly
We sprout new wings to soar on high

We leave behind our earthbound frame
And cast aside our mortal shame
No longer bound by silver cord
We snap the chain that locked the door

Dreaming

Majestic moments glazed with love
Exude the power from above
A certain truth and certain smile
Make the trials all worthwhile

Steady plodding toward the goal
Unfolding blossom of the soul
Watered with the tears of love
Warmed by pure light from above

Gathered in by tender hand
Gently plucked up from the land
Ride the free and easy breeze
Gently floating down with ease

I looked down from my lofty perch
Guided by my need to search
And spied within the earthly mirror
An image that was oh so clear

Raindrops water dusty plains
Then resurrect to clouds again
The floodgates deep within my soul
Had opened wide and made me whole

Reflected on the planet's sea
An image staring back at me
Beneath the surface I could gaze
And with a little courage raise

The hidden secrets of the deep
Reveal themselves while we're asleep
Examine with the waking mind
The nature of the laws sublime

Ask yourself who governs thee
And who determines what's to be
And in your dreaming you will know
The force that makes the fire glow

A Step Through Time

I reached within my memory
And drew you back right here with me
A distant land so long ago
Where we had been each other's foe

The soldier you were took my life
And broke the heart of widowed wife
With no mercy, with such hate
You fired the shot that sealed my fate

The soldier l was died right then
But now we've both been born again
Ironically, you are to me
What some in life call destiny

And now you make up for the loss
That fatal bullet once had caused
You're now caretaker of my life
For you're my husband, I'm your wife

I lost my soul in earth's low tide
And couldn't count the tears I've cried
And if, indeed, my prayers were heard
God felt the tears beneath the words

And if these sayings seem too vague
It isn't that we're blind
But we like any mortal here
Will see when comes the time

And so the gates to heaven be
The door that guards the mind
The angels hold the master key
That leads to love sublime

The Wave

Nature's best and nature's worst
One day we're blessed, the next we're cursed
The rainbow and the storm are one
Joined in light by Father sun

The tide swells high and ebbs so low
The eddies spin but still they know
What they are and where they've been
And if they'll ever spin again

The wave, she rushes to the shore
To find she must go back for more
And gather from the soothing sea
The push that makes these waves to be

Time

As our lives draw to an end
The mystic veil grows ever thin
Time accelerates her speed
As days fly faster by it seems

But in our youth the days dragged on
Tomorrow took so long to come
We felt our days would never end
We knew we were immortal, friend

And now the years fly quickly by
Time is transformed and we ask why
Perhaps the Lord within us cries
To be here now with open eyes

Don't wish away your life today
With many thoughts of yesterday
And to the future we will glide
By living now, eyes open wide

Like little children we shall see
The present's opportunity
Not fearful of a future day
And no regrets of yesterday

Refreshed anew with open hearts
Anticipating each new start
Awake, alive our soul's plugged in
To cosmic power deep within

Our soul's alive with energy
Connected in a dance are we
All plugged in to creative source
And every path is right on course

Epitaph

I wandered in my dreams at night
And glimpsed the netherworld
My spirit guided by a light
The light of a young girl

It turned out that the light was me
That childhood spirit lives
She taught me that my soul is free
And love gets what she gives

And someday on my headstone write
The things my soul did touch
She dances now with such delight
She sinned because she loved so much

Freedom

Spirit wanders while we sleep
And lives in other realms
The silver cord ensures we keep
Our waiting bodies warm

The mind is not contained within
A worldly structure here
But has its freedom, knows all things
And wanders free from fear

But mortal man has made a cage
And limits mind to brain
But understand our lives will change
When knowledge grabs the rein

And knowing truth becomes the guide
That goes beyond mere faith
Then all our doubts we cast aside
And stand by heaven's gate

Choice

The fog rose from the steamy moors
The people locked and bolted doors
The town awaited death's cool hand
They feared the beast that stalked the land

And upward from the wishing well
The beast came forth and cast his spell
They knew not that they conjured him
From out of darkest thoughts within

If they had only known they could
Have cast their nets on something good
They knew not that the choice was theirs
The beast was born from deep despair

So guard the port that guards the mind
Let only in the thoughts that shine
And know that wisdom from above
Shines down the only power, Love

Haunting

A banished thought crept back to me
Of things that I'd forgot
I let it slip my memory
And chose to let it drop

But yet it kept resurfacing
Unbidden from the depths
I'll have to bury it again
Retrace my faulty steps

Do not haunt me dreadful deed
I've turned my back on you
And I just forgave myself
For sins that aren't too few

So go away and don't return
To clutter up my mind
Stay 'neath conscious memory
Thee Satan, get behind

Now I'll float with buoyancy
And focus on the good
The mirrored surface of the sea
Has hid all that it could

Serendipity

Summer heat and winter rain
Brings me to my knees again
I'm but a drop in this vast sea
Clinging with tenacity
Embracing serendipity

A higher power I believe
Will heal the hearts of those that grieve
And in the twinkling of an eye
Will dry the tears of all that cry
And this I know with certainty
This secret was revealed to me
By way of serendipity

Good Luck

Luck is not a lady
I once heard someone say
Luck is what we make it
Or what we throw away

Luck's another word for God
I heard another say
Something we can win or lose
If we just learn to pray

Coincidence may be the sign
That says our choice is right
An omen that will tell us where
We're stopping for the night

Apart Together

My heart had longed to hear your voice
My soul it seemed, just had no choice
For with you I was meant to be
Although I know I must stay free

Life's many roads will twist and bend
And on the path we find a friend
We'll walk together for a while
Your face will make my face to smile

Together we may grow apart
Or we may win each other's heart
But in the final stretch we'll see
Apart we will together be

Measured on this earthly plane
We may never love again
Somehow we always have been one
Invisible, beyond the sun

Connected we will always be
For oneness is our destiny
One with all and all are one
Like Holy Father, Holy Son

Departure

My heart is like an open wound
My breath it soon will cease
I've been bitten by the lion
And shaken by the beast

The body that had housed my soul
Would soon give up the ghost
Projected from this mortal shell
To join the holy host

A host of angels gathered near
The holy veil grew thin
The silver cord is loosed on high
My soul has found its wings

Petals of Love

Deep inside the heart of the flower
And still asleep were the seeds
Awaiting their appointed hour
To awake from their dreaming sleep

It seemed the time would never come
In the journey from womb to tomb
So many and long their days in the sun
This moment seemed way too soon

Prepared so they thought, turned out they were not
And no one can know the day
When the Master will knock on the door of the heart
And scatter the seeds far away

But contained in the seed is the Master's plan
That charts each petal and leaf
To awaken one day in a new and strange land
Forgetting all sorrow and grief

Nature

Oh, morning dew, I've seen you shine
Beneath the glistening veil
And I've wondered all the time
How in the wind you sail

Oh, rhythmic rain, I've seen your dance
Upon our Mother Earth
And I've wondered all the time
The nature of your birth

Oh, brightest sun, I've felt your warmth
Upon my naked skin
And I've wondered all the time
How great the cosmic wind

Oh, gentle stars, you spill your light
With darkness all around
And I've wondered all the time
If you can make a sound

Oh, gliding bird, you aim your wings
To capture best the air
And I've wondered all the time
Just how you feel up there

Oh, glowing plants, I've seen your smile
Within your blooming flower
And I've wondered all the time
The nature of such power

Oh, sweetest Lord, you've heard our prayers
As gently they were sighed
And I've known somehow the while
You've never left my side

About the Author

This author has had a life's journey with many ups and downs and winding roads. She found a resting place of peace in prayer and meditation. It is from this place of peace that the poems have sprung. In the quietness of prayer, in one's own closet, the muddy waters clear. A new understanding may take shape and hope is not lost. On a wing and a prayer, we all journey through life, not knowing what may lie just around the bend. In a constant state of transition, life is a thread, a silver cord, that weaves together with others, and with our Maker. Each strand has its own beauty, and each is precious. Our stages of life are like the butterfly. This author is currently in the pupae stage and has not yet received her wings but hopes to share with you some of her mindful meditations before the silver cord is loosed. Read on, my dear butterfly in the making.